Teacher Representati Dramatic Text and P

T0247613

This book examines representations of the teacher on stage – in both theatrical performances and dramatic text – in order to demonstrate how these representations have shaped society's perceptions of educators in and out of the classroom.

At the heart of this book is the interaction between theatre and teacher education. By considering how dramatic portrayals reimagine, reinforce and/or undermine our understanding of the teacher's personal and professional roles, this volume bridges the gap between truth in dramatic literature and truth in the classroom. Chapters critically explore the personas embodied by fictional teachers in well-known works such as *Educating Rita, School of Rock* and *The History Boys* and illustrate how educators might use dramatic literature and performance to interrogate entrenched ideas about the student-teacher dynamic. By bringing together a diverse set of contributors from the fields of teacher education and theatre, this book takes a critical look at performance, text, society and culture to promote a new understanding of teaching and learning.

This unique book will be of great interest to graduate and postgraduate students, academics and researchers in the fields of teacher education, drama and theatre education.

Melanie Shoffner is Professor of Education at James Madison University, USA.

Richard St. Peter is Assistant Professor of Theatre at Northwestern State University, USA.

Routledge Research in Teacher Education

The Routledge Research in Teacher Education series presents the latest research on Teacher Education and also provides a forum to discuss the latest practices and challenges in the field.

Teacher Education in the Trump Era and Beyond
Preparing New Teachers in a Contentious Political Climate
Edited by Laura Baecher, Megan Blumenreich, Shira Eve Epstein and Julie R. Horwitz

Values and Professional Knowledge in Teacher Education
Nick Mead

Professional Development through Mentoring
Novice ESL Teachers' Identity Formation
Juliana Othman and Fatiha Senom

Research on Becoming an English Teacher
Through Lacan's Looking Glass
Tony Brown, Mike Dore and Christopher Hanley

Intercultural Competence in the Work of Teachers
Confronting Ideologies and Practices
Edited by Fred Dervin, Robyn Moloney and Ashley Simpson

Teacher Representations in Dramatic Text and Performance
Portraying the Teacher on Stage
Edited by Melanie Shoffner and Richard St. Peter

For more information about this series, please visit: https://www.routledge.com/Routledge-Research-in-Teacher-Education/book-series/RRTE

Teacher Representations in Dramatic Text and Performance

Portraying the Teacher on Stage

Edited by Melanie Shoffner and Richard St. Peter

Routledge
Taylor & Francis Group

NEW YORK AND LONDON

First published 2020
by Routledge
605 Third Avenue, New York, NY 10017

and by Routledge
2 Park Square, Milton Park, Abingdon, Oxon, OX14 4RN

First issued in paperback 2021

*Routledge is an imprint of the Taylor & Francis Group,
an informa business*

© 2020 Taylor & Francis

The right of Melanie Shoffner and Richard St. Peter to
be identified as the authors of the editorial material, and
of the authors for their individual chapters, has been
asserted in accordance with sections 77 and 78 of the
Copyright, Designs and Patents Act 1988.

Library of Congress Cataloging-in-Publication Data
A catalog record for this title has been requested

ISBN 13: 978-0-367-77780-7 (pbk)
ISBN 13: 978-0-367-22781-4 (hbk)

Typeset in Sabon
by codeMantra

To Anna Claspy,
Whose friendship, humor and support were greatly
appreciated from the beginning to the end of
this project.
You are indeed a wonder.
~ Melanie Shoffner

* * * * *

To my kids Olivia and Aidan,
For making me always want to be a better father.

To my teachers,
David Balthrop
Naum Panovski
Dorothy Chansky
Bill Gelber
For making me always want to be a better teacher.

And to my students,
For keeping me young.
~ Richard St. Peter

Contents

Contributors

Benny Sato Ambush holds an MFA in Directing from University of California, San Diego, and is a Fellow of the American Theatre. He is a stage director, producer and teacher of acting and directing at university programs nationally. He has served as the Senior Distinguished Producing Director-In-Residence at Emerson Stage/Emerson College; Acting Artistic Director at Rites and Reason Theatre Company; Producing Artistic Director at Oakland Ensemble Theatre; Associate Artistic Director at American Conservatory Theater; Co-Artistic Director at San Francisco Bay Area Playwrights Festival and Associate Artistic Director at Anna Deavere Smith's Institute on the Arts & Civic Dialogue at Harvard University.

Richard Corley holds an MA from Goddard College and an MFA from Illinois State University. He teaches Shakespeare and Modern Drama at University of Illinois, Chicago. He most recently directed Tennessee Williams' *Small Craft Warnings* at the Williams Festival of St. Louis and served as the conceiver and dramaturg of *Desire*, an evening of plays based on Williams' short stories, produced by The Acting Company. Richard served for seven years as the Artistic Director of Madison Repertory Theatre in Wisconsin. He is the recipient of the TCG/NEA Director Fellowship.

Marshall George is the Olshan Professor of Clinical Practice at Hunter College of the City University of New York. He is the Program Director of the EdD Program in Instructional Leadership at Hunter and teaches in the English and Literacy Teacher Education programs as well. His scholarship has focused primarily on teaching young adult literature and on the preparation of English language arts teachers.

Andrew Goodwyn is the Head of the School of Education and English Language at the University of Bedfordshire and Emeritus Professor at the University of Reading. He is currently the President of the International Federation for the Teaching of English (IFTE). His recent publications include the book *Expert Teaching: An International Perspective* (Routledge, 2016) and the co-edited book *International Perspectives on the Teaching of Literature in Schools: Global Principles and Practices* (Routledge, 2017).

Julie Gorlewski is an Associate Professor and Chair of the Department of Learning and Instruction at the University at Buffalo, The State University of New York. A former English teacher and previous editor of *English Journal*, she has published 11 books and numerous articles and book chapters.

Shelley Nowacek earned her MFA in Directing from Virginia Commonwealth University and her doctorate from the College of William and Mary. She has nearly 30 years of theatre teaching experience from the elementary school to the university level. She has written theatre curriculum for public school divisions in Virginia and Maryland and has spoken at national conferences regarding assessment and evaluation for theatre educators. She has published numerous articles regarding educational theatre programming and assessment.

Luke Rodesiler, a former high school English teacher and coach, is an Assistant Professor at Purdue University Fort Wayne. His research interests include exploring the role of popular cultures – and particularly sports culture – in the English language arts classroom, nontraditional forms of teacher professional development and media literacy education. His scholarship can be found in various book chapters and in journals that include *English Education, English Journal, Voices from the Middle* and *Language Arts*.

Lisa Scherff teaches English and AP Research at the Community School of Naples (FL). Previously, she was a professor of English education and teacher education at the University of Tennessee, the University of Alabama and Florida State University. She is coauthor, with Susan Groenke, of *Teaching YA Lit Through Differentiated Instruction* (NCTE, 2010) and coeditor of a number of books, including *The Future of English Teaching*

Worldwide: Celebrating 50 Years From the Dartmouth Conference (Routledge, 2018) and *International Perspectives on the Teaching of Literature in Schools: Global Principles and Practices* (Routledge, 2017).

Pauline Skowron Schmidt is an Associate Professor in English Education at West Chester University in West Chester, PA, where she teaches various methods courses, supervises student teachers and is the Co-Advisor of the NCTE Student Affiliate and the Director of the Pennsylvania Writing and Literature Project (PAWLP). Her research interests include using dramatic techniques and other art forms in the English classroom, as well as examining English Language Arts curriculum in terms of inclusion and diversity. She was the Young Adult Literature column editor for *English Journal* from 2013 to 2018 and Co-Chair of NCTE's Commission on Arts and Literacies (COAL) from 2011 to 2015.

Melanie Shoffner is a Professor of Education at James Madison University. She has published two edited books and numerous articles and chapters focusing on issues of teacher preparation, reflective practice and dispositional development. She is a former Fulbright Scholar to Romania, a past chair of English Language Arts Teacher Educators (ELATE) and the current editor of *English Education*.

Jeff Spanke is a former high school English teacher and current assistant professor of English at Ball State University. He teaches courses in Young Adult Literature, Rhetoric and Composition, Introduction to English Education and English Teaching methods. His current scholarship examines the various social constructions of teachers, students and learning with a focus on the intersections of resistance and vulnerability in the education process.

James Stillwaggon's work seeks to describe the emergence of subjectivity through the public structures that give it shape and draws on continental philosophy, psychoanalysis, popular film and literature. Recent projects include a symposium of papers on melancholia and education in *Educational Theory*, a special issue on formative justice for *Teachers College Record*, and *Filmed School: Desire, Transgression and the Filmic Fantasy of Pedagogy*.

Richard St. Peter is an Assistant Professor of Theatre at Northwestern State University of Louisiana. He holds an MFA from Virginia Commonwealth University and a PhD from Texas Tech University. He is an award-winning director who has directed nearly 50 plays throughout the United States and Europe, a former Fulbright Scholar to Romania, a Visiting Lecturer at London's Rose Bruford College of Theatre and Performance and a 2002 recipient of a Princess Grace Foundation Theater Award. He is also a former college baseball player who played on traveling teams and in adult leagues until he was 37 years old.

Heather Welch is a part-time faculty member in the Department of Theatre at Bridgewater State University where she teaches courses in Theatre History, Feminist Theatre, and Theatre and Film. She is currently an advanced doctoral candidate in Fine Arts (Theatre) at Texas Tech University. Her research focuses on theatre history in the United States, primarily from the late nineteenth century to present, and the relationship between the early feminist movement and the theatricality of protest.

James Wilson is a Professor of English and Theatre at LaGuardia Community College and the Graduate Center of the City University of New York. His areas of research include queer theater and performance, African American theatre and pedagogy. He is the author of *Bulldaggers, Pansies, and Chocolate Babies: Performance, Race, and Sexuality in the Harlem Renaissance* (2010).

Foreword

Clay McLeod Chapman

Mrs. Royer. Mrs. Baugher. Mr. Raimist. Mr. Burke. Mr. Moyer. Mrs. Belov. Mrs. Arnold.

These names will mean nothing to you. They remain abstract. Anonymous.

And yet, for me, these names are everything.

Absolutely everything.

These are the teachers who I had the good fortune to intersect with during my own tumultuous time as a student. No matter how terrible of a pupil I was – and believe me, I was – these teachers had an ever-lasting impact on me. They challenged me, provoked me, pushed and prodded me. They collectively had a hand in molding me into the creative individual I am today.

I never made it easy for them. Imagine the kid in the back of the classroom, looking anywhere except for the blackboard. The daydreamer. The eye-roller. The smarmy inquisitor. The class clown.

I had the grades to prove it. Nobody would ever pin me for an honor roll student. And yet, against all odds, there was a glimmer. Some infinitesimal flicker of hope.

Of potential.

Mrs. Royer saw it first. God bless her. I was failing her class – this was 6th grade English, mind you – with very few prospects of passing and making my way to 7th grade. Whatever lesson plan was happening at the front of the classroom held no wonder for me. The words were always lost in the miasma of my own imagination, luring my attention out the window or just on the other side of the fiberglass ceiling tiles above my head. Anywhere but the chalkboard. At the rate my GPA was going, I would be sitting at the same exact desk next year.

So Mrs. Royer struck a deal with me.

She challenged me to write a story. Put that daydreaming to good use. There just-so-happened to be a new statewide competition for burgeoning playwrights seeking out submissions at the time and she suggested I enter. If I were to submit something of my own, she'd dole out some extra credit. Bump that failing grade up a numeral or two.

I was desperate to crawl out of my own self-imposed sinkhole. I was not going to be stranded in the 6th grade for another year.

And I, being the duplicitous young man that I was, figured the more plays I submitted, the more extra credit I would get... So I took to my grandparent's typewriter and banged out the most atrocious doggerel my twelve-year-old imagination could come up with.

Shakespeare, this was not...but I got my extra credit. I passed 6th grade English. I was on my way to 7th grade and that was supposed to be the end of this story.

Then I got a letter in the mail.

Congratulations, your play has been selected as one of...

To this day, I'm still haunted by the prospect of some other turn of events, some other potential timeline where Mrs. Royer hadn't challenged me to put my overactive imagination to good use. Whatever she saw in me, I can't even fathom. How deep that shimmer of creativity must have been, buried somewhere within this apathetic problem child – I never sensed it. Never felt I had that potential for something other. Something better. Something special.

I wasn't the only one who couldn't see it. Let's not list off all the other teachers who had written me off, who couldn't be bothered, who merely hit their marks to make their way through their lesson plan. Another day, another problem student. Not every teacher can be That Teacher.

Sometimes they are like Bruce Bechdel in *Fun Home*.

Or Ty Fletcher in *Tamer of Horses*.

Or Hector in *The History Boys*.

And yet, somehow, Mrs. Royer sensed it even when the rest of us couldn't. When I couldn't. She unearthed it, practically in opposition to the academic status quo. I could have so easily been another brick in the wall...but Mrs. Royer didn't let me slip. Not on her watch.

It is safe to say that I wouldn't be writing this foreword had it not been for her.

Where would I be now? Would someone else have seen that potential within me, even when I couldn't? Would someone else have tapped into it, uprooted it?

Who would I be without her?

My story isn't exceptional beyond the fact that it's my story. You have your own story about That Teacher. We all do. They were there in grade school. In high school. In college.

We carry these teachers with us for the rest of our lives. Those teachers who made an impact on us, who embedded their ideals, their guidance, within us, who follow us for the rest of our lives. The DNA of their teachings is something we carry on.

Sometimes, it's simply one. Others are blessed with several. But what is most confounding is how these teachers – whoever they may be, wherever and whenever it is that you intersect with them – will never know the impact they had. This is due primarily to the notion that we ourselves are never truly aware of their influence until years later, well after our time with them has passed. The echo of their teaching takes time to resonate.

Where is Mrs. Royer now?

What I find most compelling about the book in your hands now is that it asks one to consider the Teacher. By exploring how this figure is represented onstage, I anticipate the reader won't be able to help but reflect upon those teachers who made an impact on their own lives. I couldn't. This book called them up for me. It manifested them all over again.

Did we learn from a teacher as dynamic as Dewey Finn in *School of Rock*?

Did we change through a mentor like Frank in *Educating Rita*?

Did we play ball for a coach like Don in *Rounding Third*?

Class is in session yet again. Here they are, my teachers, still to this day…

Mrs. Baugher.

Mr. Raimist.

Mr. Burke.

They never left.

For over ten years now, I have had the good fortune of teaching. I distinctly remember that first year – how terrified I was. Who was I, some thirty-odd years old at the time, to think I could stand in front of this group of MFA students and teach them something? Anything?

Who did I think I was?

A teacher?

That hallowed distinction was reserved for those who could move intellectual mountains. Break through those cerebral barriers and achieve higher learning.

That wasn't me. It couldn't be me. I felt like I was cast in a role well beyond my range. The audience would see right through me. When I entered the stage, I was absolutely petrified my students – my students – would rip me to shreds. Eat me up.

Or perhaps simply demand their money back.

I wanted to be a teacher like Mrs. Royer. Like my own college professor, Mrs. Arnold. I wanted teaching to matter the way it had to them. To love it. To imbue that love to my students. To show them we were in this together. This journey of self-discovery.

It remains to be seen who I am in the eyes of my students, but I will say this...

You never know who That Teacher will be.

Your Teacher.

But I know who my Teachers are. Their teachings resonate just as loudly as they did when I first intersected with them. They go beyond their own lesson plans.

Say their names with me.

Mr. Moyer.

Mrs. Belov.

Mrs. Arnold.

Or, better yet – call out your own. Who were those teachers in your life that left their imprint?

Say their names. Call them up. Sing their praises over and over again, loud enough that they might hear.

Remember them.

Introduction

Melanie Shoffner and Richard St. Peter

While this book is a logical outgrowth of Melanie's edited collection *Exploring Teachers in Fiction and Film: Saviors, Scapegoats and Schoolmarms* (Shoffner, 2016), the genesis of the project was purely serendipitous. In 2016–2017, while serving as Fulbright Scholars in Romania, we had many conversations about our respective backgrounds in education and theatre and the commonalities between our fields. One day, Rick mentioned an article that looked at depictions of teachers on stage (Miss Trunchbull, 2017); Melanie mused that these portrayals were another form of public pedagogy (Giroux, 2001) – and the spark was there.

This book considers what we learn from dramatic representations of teachers. Anchor chapters examine the teachers depicted by playwrights, directors and actors; response chapters delve into specific elements of those examinations. By writing about, structuring and embodying teachers on the stage, those connected to the theatre offer a specific version of the teacher to the public. In response, by considering what that understanding means beyond the stage, those connected to education offer a singular viewpoint on issues relevant to modern education.

At the heart of this book is the interaction between theatre and teacher education. This book attempts to bridge the gap between truth in dramatic literature and truth in the classroom. What can we learn from the conversations between those who depict teachers on the stage and those who prepare teachers for the classroom, between those who present teachers and those who represent teachers? Together, the authors in this book create a cross-disciplinary dialogue that offers a nuanced consideration of what we take away, consciously or not, when we see teachers under the lights of the stage.

Rick's View From the Stage

The essence of drama is conflict. What better medium than the theatre to play out the ongoing battles faced in education? In that fateful *Guardian* (2017) article depicting memorable teachers on stage, the teachers' character is described in vividly descriptive language: Miss Trunchbull is "monstrous" in *Matilda the Musical*; Andrew-Crocker Harris is "unlikeable" in *The Browning Version*. Actors walk on stage to play teachers who embody conflict: Alan Rickman as Leonard is a "bad tempered tutor" in *Seminar*; Nikki Amuka-Bird as Ms. Evitt faces a classroom mutiny in *God Bless the Child*.

Teaching often engenders a clash over ideals and ideology; moving people from ignorance to enlightenment can be a battlefield fraught with casualties. When you add issues as far-ranging as class, race, religion, even athletics – all addressed in the following chapters – to the battlefield of education, you have subjects rife for dramatic exploration.

There is a performative quality to teaching. A teacher is, in essence, an actor, learning a script – the lesson plan, the interactions with students, the route through the hallways – in order to deliver a convincing performance. The teacher takes on a role – the knowledgeable scholar, the creative innovator, the laidback rule-breaker – and attempts to deliver it successfully to diverse watchers. Actors do the same. A play, like a lesson, doesn't truly come alive until an actor breathes spirit into the words. The stage becomes the actor's classroom as the audience settles into its space. What do they learn from Antigone's dilemma? Lysistrata's? Juliet's?

Theatre, as a communal artform, truly does hold a mirror up to society and in doing so allows society to have an ongoing conversation with itself. What does that conversation entail when the stage is given over to the realm of the teacher? More importantly, how well do playwrights, actors and directors depict teachers on stage? Does a playwright have an obligation to faithfully render the role of teacher or can the teacher serve merely as a kind of cipher for the playwright to explore larger societal issues? If the goal of the theatre is both profit and delight, what can be learned from the teachers presented in the following chapters?

As a director, my obligation is to communicate the truths found in a text to the audience there to see a production. Working with playwrights and actors, my first responsibility is to articulate those truths and breathe life into them through the *mise-en-scène* of the play. It is not *real* life; it is *dramatic* life. At best, it is a heightened version of life. As such, there can be a tunnel vision when working in the theatre, but I would argue we strive to get correct the heightened version of the subjects we put on stage. Is that the case with teachers? Do we get it right?

Maybe one area of commonality that can be found between teachers and actors is the common misperception that either profession is "real work" but rather something anyone can do; all that is required is passion. Teachers get summers off. Actors are just playing. How difficult can either job be? This gross misperception overlooks the rigorous training required to truly master each discipline. How important, then, it is to have a conversation across these disciplines and connect the view from the stage to the view from the classroom.

Melanie's View From the Classroom

Theatre and education have a long-standing connection when it comes to curriculum. English language arts teachers delve into issues of female power in Euripides' *Medea* and Sophocles' *Antigone*. History teachers explore the connections between Miller's depiction of the Salem witch trials in *The Crucible* and McCarthy's Congressional hearings in the 1950s. Drama teachers adapt popular sci-fi movies for the high school stage to "put on a great play for the kids, just get them out, stage front" (Itzkoff, 2019).

The theatre also offers perspectives on teachers' work. One common metaphor used in connection to teachers is that of 'sage on the stage' (Morrison, 2014), one who holds the student audience in thrall while lecturing on their content. As education has moved away from that teacher-centered view of instruction, so, too, has the metaphor moved to that of 'guide on the side' – which also holds a view of the teacher inspired by the theatre. Now, the teacher stands in the wings, directing from a distance, encouraging students as they learn to go it alone.

Acknowledged or not, teachers play many different roles when they walk into the classroom, each in response to what the student and subject need from them. New teachers are told to act like they know what they're doing as they get their pedagogical feet under them – 'fake it until you make it' – and assume personas that may make life in the classroom easier as they adjust to their new profession – 'don't smile until Christmas.'

Yet, for all these connections, one consideration not commonly explored is the presentation of teachers on the stage – teachers on television, in film, through books (e.g., Bulman, 2002; Dalton, 2010, 2005; Harris, 2009; Joseph & Burnaford, 2001; Liston & Renga, 2014; Shaw & Nederhouser, 2005; Shoffner, 2016; Stillwaggon & Jelinek, 2017; Trier, 2001; Weber & Mitchell, 1995) but not those found in the floodlights.

In 2001, Giroux analyzed film as a form of public pedagogy, calling it "a visual technology that functions as a powerful teaching machine that intentionally tries to influence the production of meaning, subject positions, identities, and experience" (p. 587). Combining both entertainment and politics, Giroux (2001) explained that film was a site of "educated hopes and hyper-mediated experiences that connect the personal and the social by bridging the contradictory and overlapping relations between private discourses and public life" (p. 588).

When it comes to representations of teachers on the stage, the theatre offers a particular form of public pedagogy, especially when we consider the intentionality of the space for meaning making. Like a film, the stage functions as a teaching mechanism: We are educated through the social experience of connecting to the staged presentation of a reality, privately enthralled in a public space and publicly experiencing a private moment.

Thanks to our years of schooling (Lortie, 2002), as well as our years with picture books, young adult novels, movies and television shows, we know teachers. When we see teachers strutting and fretting for hours upon the stage, we embrace the familiarity, laugh at the stereotypes and smile at the memories. What we may not recognize in the moment, however, is what we have learned from those dramatic representations. How did that version of a teacher connect to our understandings of education? Why did that presentation of a teacher resonate so strongly with us but not with others in the audience? What does it mean to see that version of The Teacher?

As teachers and teacher educators, we bring another layer to that consideration of what it means to see the profession embodied on the stage. How do we react to the playwright's version of our daily lives? How do we judge the actor "playing" a fiction we inhabit as fact? How do we make sense of the director's constructed viewpoint when we operate in a particularly constructed reality? When the lights go down and the curtain comes up, we are likely lost in the magic of the theatre, but when the lights go up and the curtain comes down, we should walk away questioning what that dramatic performance means for our understanding of teachers and teaching.

The Coming Discussion

The chapters in this book examine the dramatic representations of teachers in a cross-section of plays from two different perspectives: theatre professionals and teacher educators. The common ground in this book is its focus on the staged teacher as a human being. Representations though these dramatic versions may be, these teachers are examined as real people, with emotions, actions and consequences far beyond their classrooms. We are asked to consider what we take away from these staged encounters and what we learn about teachers in those dramatic moments.

Issues on the stage often reflect current issues in society, as does the opening chapter by James Wilson. His look at "teacher panic" plays focuses on those in the 1930s–1940s that revolved around the idea of "unfit" teachers corrupting young impressionable pupils with their overt sexual proclivities. He examines the "unfit" teachers in two great twentieth-century American plays – Hellman's *The Children's Hour* and Williams' *A Streetcar Named Desire* – and one arguably forgotten play, Winsloe's *Girls in Uniform*. Against these period representations, he juxtaposes Bennett's modern teacher from the 2006 play *The History Boys*, who is unarguably problematic yet pedagogically progressive. In her chapter, Heather Welch steps away from current issues while exploring the ramifications of a potentially unfit teacher in another 2006 play: *Fun Home: The Musical*. Welch focuses on the character of Bruce Bechdel, a high school English teacher whose inability to reconcile his sexual identity has consequences for his daughter, his family and his students.

In their responses to these chapters, James Stillwaggon and Marshall George consider what these decidedly negative teacher representations mean for the audience. Stillwaggon posits that Wilson's examination of these transgressive teachers resonates with us because we are drawn to the embodiment of desire personified in these fictional teachers. George moves beyond the fictional to identify the factual in his response. With Welch's consideration of Bruce Bechdel offering little in the way of a positive teacher portrayal, George examines how using the "teacher as coach" metaphor counters Bechdel's negative characteristics while offering an understanding of a "fit" teacher.

Richard St. Peter takes up the idea of the teacher as a literal coach in his chapter's examination of two Little League coaches in Dresser's *Rounding Third* (2002). Their competing philosophies on competition echo differing philosophies in education; as they negotiate conflict on the baseball diamond, they are offering lessons on success, failure, friendship and fun. Richard Corley also looks at the different lessons learned from a somewhat unconventional teacher in his examination of mentorship in Russell's *Educating Rita* (1980). Corley's chapter explores how Frank's mentorship of Rita is an education for both of them, one that is not without its issues but one that encourages the audience to consider the shaping influences of class, gender and power.

Andrew Goodwyn and Luke Rodesiler also encourage the audience to consider different perspectives in their responses to these chapters. Goodwyn moves us away from Corley's examination of Frank and Rita on stage to the play's examination of education in life. Drawing connections to literature, myth and curriculum, Goodwyn considers how the play's depiction of teacher and student endures because of its educational resonance. In similar fashion, Rodesiler moves beyond St. Peter's examination of the coach-cum-teacher in one play to interrogate the educational role of coaches in several young adult novels. Like St. Peter, Rodesiler agrees that the coach is indeed a teacher and turns a critical eye on the educational implications of coaches' interactions with their athletes-cum-students.

In their chapters, Pauline Skowron Schmidt and Benny Sato Ambush also turn a critical eye on unconventional teachers. Schmidt focuses on Dewey Finn's "fake" teacher in Webber, Slater and Fellowes' *School of Rock: The Musical* (2015). Despite taking a substitute teaching position without any educational credentials, Schmidt argues that Finn demonstrates qualities, beliefs and outcomes that position him as a real – and effective – teacher in the classroom. Ambush's chapter examines a teacher outside his classroom in Mastrosimone's play *Tamer of Horses* (1998). Examining the interactions between Ty, an out-of-work teacher, and Hector, an illiterate juvenile delinquent, Ambush presents the teacher ethos of selfless devotion.

Lisa Scherff and Shelley Nowacek use their responses to interrogate the real-world implications of these dramatic teachers. Scherff considers how Schmidt's examination of Dewey Finn encourages us to interrogate the implications of his portrayal. Accepting such fictionalized teachers as fact, Scherff argues, ignores the complex, demanding reality of teaching in K-12 schools today. Likewise,

Nowacek takes issue with Ambush's acceptance of the selfless teacher in his analysis of *Tamer of Horses*. In her response, she instead offers Ty as representative of the teacher savior, presenting him as an idealized version of the selfless teacher when he is really selfish and self-serving.

The book concludes with Jeff Spanke's chapter on Shanley's *Doubt*, which explores conflicts of identity, calling and purpose among teachers in a Catholic school. As do the other authors, Spanke considers the human-ness of teachers who find themselves caught up by concerns that reach beyond the classroom, as they question their pedagogical beliefs, their communal interactions and their educative purposes. In her response, Julie Gorlewski builds on Spanke's considerations of doubt, belief and integrity by stressing the importance of struggling with such complex issues. Teachers must grapple with conflict in order to build a future that embraces equity and justice in education.

In this book, we, too, have grappled with the conflict of dramatic representation of teachers on the stage. Education represents one of the basic tenets of the social contract; teachers remain fertile ground for dramatists wishing to interrogate the ongoing validity of that contract. Race, religion, politics, class and sexuality are all ideas that find their way into classrooms and, as long as teachers are wrestling with these issues, playwrights are dramatizing their struggle. The theatre and the classroom: two mirrors capable of showing society the same reflection.

References

Bulman, R. C. (2002). Teachers in the 'hood: Hollywood's middle-class fantasy. *The Urban Review*, 34(3), 251–276.

Dalton, M. M. (2005). Our Miss Brooks: Situating gender in teacher sitcoms. In M. M. Dalton, & L. R. Linder (Eds.), *The sitcom reader: America viewed and skewed* (pp. 99–110). New York: State University of New York Press.

Dalton, M. M. (2010). *The Hollywood curriculum: Teachers in the movies*. New York: Peter Lang.

From Miss Trunchbull to Mr Chips: Top teachers on stage – In pictures. (2017, April 24). *The Guardian*. Retrieved from https://www.theguardian.com/us

Giroux, H. (2001). Breaking into the movies: Pedagogy and the politics of film. *JAC: A Journal of Composition Theory*, 21(3), 583–598.

Harris, A. (2009). The good teacher: Images of teachers in popular culture. *English Drama Media*, 14, 11–18.

Itzkoff, D. (2019, March 25). High school "Alien" production wins internet raves. *The New York Times*. Retrieved from https://www.nytimes.com

Joseph, P. B., & Burnaford, G. E. (2001). *Images of schoolteachers in America*. Mahwah, NJ: Lawrence Erlbaum.

Liston, D. P., & Renga, I. (Eds.). (2014). *Teaching, learning, and school in film: Reel education*. New York: Routledge.

Lortie, D. C. (2002). *Schoolteacher: A sociological study* (2nd ed.). Chicago, IL: University of Chicago Press.

Morrison, Ch. D. (2014). From "sage on the stage" to "guide on the side": A good start. *International Journal for the Scholarship of Teaching and Learning, 8*(1), 1–15.

Shaw, C. C., & Nederhouser, D. D. (2005). Reel teachers: References for reflection for real teachers. *Action in Teacher Education, 27*(3), 85–94.

Shoffner, M. (Ed.). (2016). *Exploring teachers in fiction and film: Saviors, scapegoats and schoolmarms*. New York: Routledge.

Stillwaggon, J., & Jelinek, D. (2017). *Filmed school: Desire, transgression and the filmic fantasy of pedagogy*. New York: Routledge.

Trier, J. (2001). The cinematic representation of the personal and professional lives of teachers. *Teacher Education Quarterly, 28*(3), 127–142.

Weber, S., & Mitchell, C. (1995). *"That's funny, you don't look like a teacher": Interrogating images, identity and popular culture*. New York: Routledge.

1 Unfit to Teach
Morality, Panic and Hazardous Teachers

James Wilson

Of the many reasons expressed by school boards and superintendents to terminate a teacher from her position, one of the most unusual might relate to the case of Marguerite S. Cunningham. In 1940, Mrs. Cunningham, a 51-year-old New York City fifth-grade teacher, was pronounced physically unfit for her job. Weighing 275 pounds and using a cane for walking, Mrs. Cunningham, according to the education board president, was "bound to slow up the exit from school in case of emergency" and, therefore, was a "fire hazard" ("275-Pound Teacher," 1940). To demonstrate her probable obstruction in a crisis, the board conducted an unannounced fire drill, strategically placing board members as witnesses: "Before Mrs. Cunningham had limped down the stairs," the chairman concluded, "the children in her class were a block away from her" ("Special Fire Drill," 1940). The press did not publish the final ruling but Mrs. Cunningham became the prime symbol to root out physically and mentally unsound teachers. A year after the Cunningham-induced fire drill, Governor Herbert Lehman signed into law a bill "requiring New York City teachers to submit to an examination as to their physical and mental capacity, if such an examination was directed by the Superintendent of Schools" ("Special Fire Drill," 1940). As Mrs. Cunningham's case exemplifies, teaching effectiveness often had little to do with teachers' command of subject matter or their ability to impart knowledge but with their bodily and psychological fitness.

As a result of Progressive reform in the early twentieth century, more and more students were going to (and staying in) school. Education historian Diane Ravitch (2001) explains that, in 1900, about 10 percent of all teenagers were enrolled in high school; by 1940, this number had reached about 70 percent. This increased democratization of education, along with a fixation on physical and mental suitability as an American ideal, caused a series of panics as communities turned over greater control of their young to teachers. The anxiety, in turn, triggered intensified surveillance of teacher bodies, comportment and extracurricular behavior (see, for example, Perrillo, 2004). The lives of the students, alarmists argued, depended on it.

In 1929, New York's Board of Education reported that a teacher was "under an obligation to look after his own [physical and mental] health, not only to increase his efficiency, but to set an example of an 'ideal of healthy adulthood'" ("Health of Teachers"). Dr. Sara Geiger reported to the American Psychiatric Association that a major cause of juvenile delinquency was related to unfit teachers, who had been attracted to the profession "because of short hours and long vacations, or a desire to dominate, which has never been gratified" ("Child Delinquency," 1938). She also claimed administrators did not effectively weed out the large number who were morally and mentally unfit for working with youth. Therefore, in an era in which the physical and moral health of young men and women was the country's most valued commodity, teachers were perceived as a potential national threat.

Since the 1920s, there have been many plays that reflect this obsession with unfit teachers. This chapter focuses on *teacher panic* plays, dramas that depict teachers who pose moral, physical or psychological dangers to students. While real-life teachers were regularly identified by their presumed physical unhealthiness and bodily excesses, stage teachers were marked by their equally presumed mental unhealthiness and sexual excesses. Historically, many plays, such as Philo Higley and Philip Dunning's *Remember the Day* (1935) and John Boruff's *Bright Boy* (1944), present gentle teachers; other plays, such as Clifford Goldsmith's *What a Life* (1938) and *Schoolhouse on the Lot* (1938), portray teachers as innocuously ridiculous. There are a few heroic and self-sacrificing teachers, most notably Miss Moffatt from *The Corn is Green* (1940), but there are substantially more characters who typify psychological malevolence, sadism and uncontrollable sexual desires. Additionally, these plays often depict schools and colleges as corrupt and noxious environments, and many demonstrate the dangers morally unstable educators pose to students. These plays exhibit the need for managing and disciplining the morally and sexually hazardous teachers among the ranks.

"Revolting! A Scandal! A Scandal!"

The most successful teacher play of the interwar period was Lillian Hellman's *The Children's Hour*, which opened in November 1934.

When it closed 690 performances later, it was the ninth longest running production in Broadway's history. The drama incorporates many of the hallmarks of a teacher panic play, especially in the alarm caused by a possible lesbian teacher amidst young girls, and, as with most plays of the period (and succeeding periods as well, for that matter), the putatively sexually deviant character is destroyed. As Schildcrout (2014) notes, for example, many plays depicted lesbian, gay, bisexual and transexual (LGBT) characters as murderers, tragic victims and objects of ridicule.

The central teacher characters are Karen Wright and Martha Dobie, who oversee a New England school for girls. Both women are unmarried but Karen is engaged to Joe Cardin, a local doctor. In the beginning, Martha is disheartened by the possible marriage since this could mean the end of their (presumably, professional) partnership. From there, the plot, which revolves around a series of threats, libelous whispers and eventual ruination of the school and teachers, is set into motion when some of the children overhear Martha's aunt, the meddling Lily Mortar, tell Martha that her possessiveness of Karen is "unnatural. Just as unnatural as it can be" (Hellman, 1981, p. 21). At the end, Martha shoots herself after admitting she is the unmentionable and unnamed thing Mary Tilford, the malevolent child, accuses her of being.

Although fictional, the Wright-Dobie school presents a familiar portrait of a girls' boarding school of the early twentieth century. As the curtain rises, the students are sewing, doing each other's hair and practicing elocution. As Blount (2005) shows, schools and colleges often required students to take hygiene classes, which "reinforced traditional gender behaviors and sexual practices" (p. 72). While boarding schools trained girls to be upstanding (heterosexual) women, these institutions were also suspiciously regarded as potential sites in which same-sex crushes and passions might ignite. Girls were thought to be especially prone to homosexuality, and one of the reasons for this, as noted sociologist Willard Waller argued in 1932, had to do with a belief that female genitalia are "less complex" than males' and, therefore, less specific in their "sexual aims" (p. 140). Physicians in the United States made similar claims, and building on the work of noted British sexologist Havelock Ellis at the turn-of-the-century, they proclaimed, "Female boarding schools and colleges are the great breeding grounds of artificial [acquired] homosexuality" (as cited in Blount, 2005, p. 34).

When *The Children's Hour* opened on Broadway, several critics noted its similarities with another play that dealt with lesbianism at a girls' boarding school, Christa Winsloe's *Girls in Uniform* (1932), adapted from the German play *Gersten Und Heute*. Though not actually a teacher panic play, since the focus is on a student's possible lesbianism, it is relevant here, for it reflects prevalent attitudes about teachers, students and sexual desires. *Girls in Uniform* tells the story of Manuela, a motherless girl who falls in love with her teacher, Fräulein von Bernburg. While the headmistress and other teachers are cruel, or at the very least cold, with the girls and other women faculty, Fräulein von Bernburg is motherly with her charges. She accuses the headmistress of fostering the school's pervasive sadism: "You kill the soul, the spirit! This galvanised suppression is spiritual death. Only women can do such terrible things to women!" (Winsloe, 1936, p. 129) Fräulein von Bernburg, on the other hand, kisses each girl goodnight, and when she discovers that Manuela's underwear is rife with holes (in a scene pulsating with homoeroticism), she offers one of her own chemises. Feeling empowered one evening, wearing her teacher's chemise and having accidentally gotten drunk on spiked punch, Manuela publicly proclaims her love for her teacher in front of her schoolmates and headmistress. "Revolting! A scandal! A scandal!," (Winsloe, 1936, p. 93), the headmistress declares, and Manuela is sentenced to permanent isolation. After a tearful goodbye with Fräulein von Bernburg, Manuela exits, and moments later she throws herself out of a window to her death.

Both *The Children's Hour* and *Girls in Uniform* present girls' boarding schools as breeding grounds for pestilential homosexuality. In Hellman's play, as soon as Mrs. Tilford understands the accusation Mary whispers in her ear (because it is so horrific it cannot be mentioned aloud), the grandmother informs the other parents and guardians. Within hours, the school is evacuated, and the teachers confront Mrs. Tilford, who defiantly states, "I have done what I had to do. What [Karen and Martha] are may possibly be their own business. It becomes a great deal more than that when children are concerned in it" (Hellman, 1981, p. 47). Similarly, Fräulein von Kesten, the headmistress of *Girls in Uniform*, orders Manuela's removal from physical and social contact from her peers: "The other children must run no further risk of contamination" (Winsloe, 1936, p. 105). As a result of drunken pseudo-confession and whispered accusation, Manuela, Karen and Martha are regarded as outcasts and pathological criminals. Such a response would not have been unusual in actual educational settings.

Homosexuality, according to the beliefs at the time, was considered a social disease and strong precautions were suggested for guarding oneself from contact with a known homosexual. In his classic study *The Sociology of Teaching* (1932), Waller states definitively, "For nothing seems more certain than that homosexuality is contagious," and he suggests measures for strict screening of "latent or active" homosexual teachers (pp. 144–145). According to most contemporary sources, children were principally susceptible. Education leaders warned of schoolgirl crushes, which as intimated in *Girls in Uniform*, could result in tragedy and/or lesbianism if not nipped in the bud. Johnson (1939), a school psychologist, provided a series of pointers for dealing with teacher-student infatuations to prevent long-term social maladjustment, warning,

> If the older woman is herself of the homosexual type and encourages and reciprocates the girl's affection great harm may be done the girl by causing her to select one of her own sex as the object of her love.
>
> (p. 533)

Caution and thoughtfulness, she concludes, must be taken to assure the girl's "normal development of heterosexuality" (p. 533).

"This Woman Is Morally Unfit for Her Position"

The figure of the immoral teacher remains an enduring image in plays of the 1920s through the 1940s. Homosexuality was not the only transgression: heterosexual teachers preying on students was also a familiar topic. These plays often show the ways in which teachers and professors use their positions of power to dominate young and vulnerable lives. Plays about heterosexual male teachers and professors behaving badly include Paul Osborn's *Hotbed* (1928), which involves a college rhetoric instructor who is having a dalliance with a young co-ed; Irving Stone's *Truly Valiant* (1936), which focuses on a college professor who impregnates a young student boarder, putting his textbook deal into jeopardy; and *The Druid Circle* (1947) by John Van Druten, a play about a bitter and cruel college professor who perversely humiliates a pair of student lovers. In all of these examples, the harm the teachers and professors inflict is secondary to the possible damage the controversies may have on their careers and schools.

Arguably the most famous morally and mentally unfit schoolteacher to appear on stage is Blanche DuBois from Tennessee Williams's *A Streetcar Named Desire* (1947). Blanche claims to have left her high school English teaching job as a result of fatigue and anxiety over losing Belle Reve, the family home. She explains to Stella, "I was so exhausted by all I'd been through my – nerves broke. [...] So Mr. Graves – Mr. Graves is the high school superintendent – he suggested I take a leave of absence" (Williams, 2004, p. 14). She actually became involved with a 17-year-old male student, however, and when the superintendent finds out from the student's father, she is terminated. As Stanley explains, "They told her she better move on to some fresh territory. Yep, it was practickly a town ordinance passed against her!" (Williams, 2004, p. 123). Her affair with the young man is, according to the characters who debase her, a symptom of her sexual insatiability and her unchecked sexual desire eventually leads to an emotional and psychological breakdown.

As Leibman (1987) argues, Blanche is a victim of her own sexuality and she is "punished with insanity for expressing [her] desire" (p. 27). Blanche is considered especially immoral because she is linked with homosexuality (having married Allen, a gay man, and impelled his suicide) and teenagers (evident in her scene with the newspaper boy). Guilt over Allen's death and loneliness drive Blanche to moral unfitness and she uses the cover of spinsterhood. She confesses to Mitch,

> Yes, I had many intimacies with strangers. After the death of Allen—intimacies with strangers was all I seemed able to fill my empty heart with...I think it was panic, just panic, that drove me from one to another, hunting for some protection—here and there, in the most—unlikely places—even, at last, in a seventeen-year-old boy.
>
> (Williams, 2004, p. 146)

Blanche epitomizes the sexually deviant school teacher trope. On the surface, she is respectable, spouting poetry and speaking pristine (southern) English. She refers to herself as an "old maid school teacher" (Williams, 2004, p. 60) and she recoils from anything reeking of commonness or prurience. However, the chinks in her armor are clear early on, such as the need for excessive alcohol to calm her nerves (Williams, 2004, p. 11), but she hides behind the cover of professional and personal respectability. Not unlike a vampire, Blanche is dependent on young people to maintain her own youthfulness. In exchange for wisdom and verses, Blanche desires emotional comfort and recaptured innocence. She tells Mitch that when she lost her job, "My youth was suddenly gone up the water-spout" (Williams, 2004, p. 147). Students and strangers offer provisional sustenance but Blanche pays a high price for satisfying her attempts to hold onto passing time.

Teachers, particularly women in the profession, were expected to be sexually inactive and disinterested, thus the legal prohibition on married teachers in many communities through the 1930s. Yet schools are often imagined as places for innocent romances and harmless crushes among the students; Blanche alludes to this when she tells Mitch that her attempts to engage her pupils in literary pursuits are often for naught:

> Their literary heritage is not what most of them treasure above all else! But they're sweet things! And in the spring, it's touching to notice them making their first discovery of love! As if nobody had ever known it before!
>
> (Williams, 2004, p. 62)

Blanche violates the presumption of an asexual woman school teacher. She eroticizes and embodies heterosexual desire, and in her affair with the 17-year-old – who is portrayed as an unwitting victim in the salacious fling – she taints and debases the fabled version of young love. As a result, the school board immediately fires her, with the rationale that "this woman is morally unfit for her position" (Williams, 2004, p. 146).

The Enduring Trope

More recently, the unfit teacher character is manifested in Alan Bennett's *The History Boys*, imported from London to Broadway with its original National Theatre cast in 2006. Richard Griffiths won acclaim for his performance of Hector, the inspirational and unconventional teacher at the center. Bennett's (2006) character description does not mention Hector's manner and appearance except to say that "Hector is a man of studied eccentricity. He wears a bowtie" (p. 4). Echoing the case of Marguerite Cunningham recounted in the introduction, the girth of Hector became a primary feature when the role became associated with Griffiths. In reviews and news stories, the character is described first and foremost by his size: He is "roly-poly English master Hector" (Rooney, 2006), and "Hector, a rotund, engaging, extremely unorthodox professor of English literature" (Riedel, 2006).

Griffiths' Hector violates the conventional and professional requirements of a physically and morally fit teacher prescribed in the early twentieth century. At more than 300 pounds, he would be considered unhealthy; he is abusive and a homosexual (if not a possible pedophile), yet, in 2006, not only were these aspects excused, they were extolled. As Ben Brantley (2006) summarized the play,

> This is a work in which the most likable and, by the play's standards, most moral figure is an obese English teacher who regularly swats his students in class and fiddles (to use the euphemism of choice) with the more attractive of them after school.

A similarly sympathetic teacher character in the United States 50 years prior is inconceivable, and one cannot imagine such a play getting past England's Lord Chamberlain in the same period. While Martha from *Children's Hour* and Blanche from *Streetcar* are punished and destroyed for their presumably deviant sexual desires, Hector's proclivity for fondling the boys is simply a quirk in his personality.

Indeed, *The History Boys*'s success depends on overturning audience expectations and, simultaneously, upturns assumptions about physically and morally fit schoolteachers. As with other inspirational teachers from theatre and film, Hector is uninterested in rote learning, course grades and honors certificates – or what he calls, "those longed-for emblems of your conformity" (Bennett, 2006, p. 4). He intends to inspire the boys, give them the tools for absorbing and embodying knowledge, and he provides them with the ability to make the most of every moment they are living (rather than the ability to merely make a living). His unconventionality is what makes this possible. Even in a much more gay-accepting society, it seems implausible Hector would get away with his swatting, fiddling and tossing aside A-level prep lessons (especially in the socially conservative Thatcher and Reagan 1980s in which the play is set), but the play manages to brush aside the implications of Hector's supposed molestation. First, Hector's fondling of the boys is never shown on stage: the audience must concoct an image of a contortionist driving a motorcycle with one hand. Second, the boys willingly take the ride. The director and cast grappled with this issue in rehearsal and concluded,

> In the hands of a different playwright, the image of a teacher touching his students' genitals would be sinister, if not downright disturbing, but in *The History Boys* it becomes a source of amusement for the boys—at least until it proves to be Hector's undoing and the end of his teaching career.
>
> (Thirlwell, 2005, p. 10)

This suggests an Oscar Wildean ideal of education, in which a young man attains intellectual and spiritual illumination from an older man, who also bestows physical affection on the younger. The boys endure Hector's attentions as the price they pay for the unique and ostensibly life-changing education he confers. The effects are meant to be comical, even as the goals for educational enlightenment are to be taken seriously. Like Wilde, though, the trysts lead to Hector's downfall, making the play highly conventional in dealing with presumably sexual deviant characters. Hector, whether a harmless homosexual or a contemptible pedophile, is destroyed: He dies in a motorcycle accident. His rival teacher, Irwin, who is also gay, is severely punished: The same accident renders him paralyzed from the waist down. Even the one openly gay student does not fare well: As an adult he lives a life of isolation, regret and "periodic breakdowns" (Bennett, 2006, p. 108).

Conclusion

As the sampling of plays discussed here shows, school teachers remain ambivalent figures in the cultural imagination. On the one hand, teachers are often revered for their selfless devotion to their profession. The media is filled with stories of inspirational school teachers, who nurture the creativity, intellectual brilliance and social activism of prominent figures. There are, however, just as many narratives about and cultural representations of bad teachers. The large number of teacher panic plays of the last century reflects the underlying anxieties associated with the sexual and erotic power teachers have over a nation's youth. In most cases, the teacher characters are presented as oppressors who pose a genuine or fabricated threat to the morality, physical well-being and/or intellectual growth of their students. Threats to the young, after all, in political parlance constitute threats to the aspirations of society. These plays highlight the presumed power of teachers and the near-obsession with rooting out, monitoring and disciplining unfit teachers in order to regulate the moral and psychological well-being of a country's future.

References

275-pound teacher termed a "fire hazard." (1940, March 27). *New York Times.*

Bennett, A. (2006). *The history boys.* New York: Faber and Faber, Inc.

Blount, J. M. (2005). *Fit to teach: Same-sex desire, gender, and school work in the twentieth century.* Albany, NY: State University of New York Press.

Brantley, B. (2006, April 24). Rivals for young hearts and minds in Alan Bennett's "history boys." *New York Times.*

Child delinquency linked to schools. (1938, June 7). *New York Times.*

Health of teachers. (1929, August 31). *New York Times.*

Hellman, L. (1981). *The children's hour.* New York: Dramatists Play Service, Inc. (Original work published 1934, revised 1952).

Johnson, B. E. (1939). Adolescent crushes and the teacher's responsibility. *The Clearing House, 13*(9), 531–534.

Leibman, N. C. (1987). Sexual misdemeanor/ psychoanalytic felony. *Cinema Journal, 26*(2), 27–38.

Perrillo, J. (2004). Beyond "progressive" reform: Bodies, discipline, and the construction of the professional teacher in interwar America. *History of Education Quarterly, 44*(3), 337–363.

Ravitch, D. (2001). American traditions of education. In T. M. Moe (Ed.), *A primer on America's schools* (pp. 1–14). Stanford, CA: Hoover Institution Press.

Riedel, M. (2006, April 19). Back with the muggles: From Harry to "history" for Griffiths. *New York Post.*

Rooney, D. (2006, April 23). Review: "The history boys." *Variety.*

Schildcrout, J. (2014). *Murder most queer: The homicidal homosexual in the American theater.* Ann Arbor: University of Michigan Press.

Special fire drill held for teacher: It proved 275-pound woman definitely is a hazard, Mrs. Lindloff says. (1940, April 3). *New York Times.*

Thirlwell, E. (Ed.). (2005). *National theatre education: The history boys workpack.* London: The Royal National Theatre Board.

Waller, W. (1965). *The sociology of teaching.* New York: John Wiley & Sons, Inc. (Original work published 1932).

Williams, T. (2004). *A streetcar named desire.* New York: New Directions. (Original work published 1947).

Winsloe, C. (1936). *Girls in uniform.* (B. Burnham, English adaptation). Boston, MA: Little, Brown, and Company.

Response to Chapter 1
Sexual Perversity in Our Dreams of Teaching

James Stillwaggon

In "Unfit to Teach," James Wilson draws readers to a richly detailed and unsettling paradox. He proposes that the idealized teachers we create in literature as a way of representing the profession to ourselves often embody traits that are antithetical, even subversive, to the largely socially conservative function that real teachers are expected to uphold. At first glance, we might argue that all fictional characters are intended to be larger than life and that their transgressive character demonstrates the power of literature to convey a sense of what is possible rather than what is mere fact. But literary renderings of other professions tend to produce heroic and noble expressions of human potential, whereas in the case of teachers, Wilson suggests that our best known fictional representatives are more often our most infamous, embodying desires and beliefs that challenge and even contradict the social norms that form their historical context.

The paradox that Wilson details is no small matter. On the one hand, the emotional investments that we, as a public, make in teachers as a social group shape the attitudes that our children have toward their teachers. How we, as a public, feel about teachers has a direct effect on the efficacy of pedagogy, or the value that children place on the messages that teachers deliver. On the other hand, the "ideal of healthy adulthood" (Wilson, 2019, p. 10) that we expect of teachers remains central to the content of curricula, insofar as teachers remain some of our children's earliest models of robust and flourishing citizenry outside the home. If children are the arrows shot from our bows into some unknowable future, the publicly shared fantasies we maintain about teachers determine not only how far our children might fly but also in which direction.

Yet as Wilson's chapter suggests – and as a broader survey of fictional teachers in various media overwhelmingly corroborates (cf. Bauer, 1998; Chennault, 2006; Dalton, 1999; Farber, Provenzo, & Holm, 1994; Stillwaggon & Jelinek, 2016) – the kinds of teachers we celebrate in words and on stage are remarkably different from the teachers we ask for in real classrooms. Unlike Marguerite S. Cunningham, the unfortunate teacher featured in Wilson's chapter who fell victim to the trap of the fire drill, the teachers who dwell in the space of our fantasies do not fail the ideal of healthy adulthood so much as go beyond it completely. Our literary teaching heroes overshoot the demands of their profession, taking up residence in an outsiders' world not of failures but of deviants, misfits and hedonists. Instead of Willy Loman, too painfully aware of his own failure to live up to an arbitrary social standard of success, our profession is more often represented in the public imaginary by figures like Blanche DuBois and Hector, who seem to reside in a heedless breach of basic social norms, forever in pursuit of something completely beyond the respectable lives they are supposedly conferring upon their charges. If the teachers represented on the stage provide a model of adulthood, the "healthy ideal" they embody may not be immediately apparent. If we are to consider why we continually cycle back to a fantasied image of teaching as an embodiment of seemingly illicit drives, we may get the added benefit of critically revisiting the social function that real teachers are expected to serve in reproducing social norms.

A clear place to start thinking about the relationship between teachers and illicit fantasies is in the socially conservative function teachers' work plays in reproducing social norms in the future much as they have been realized in the past. As Dewey (1944) argues, biological reproduction provides a necessary condition for humanity, but the realization of our human potential through those social habits that we designate as distinctly human depends upon languages, skills and a host of other learned practices transmitted from one generation to the next through educative practices. In other words, at their best and their worst, teachers engage in a culturally procreative relationship with their students that complements the heteronormative relations of sexual reproduction, breathing spirit into the clay of human materiality by engaging students in the discursive world to which they have been belatedly born. While we expect ordinary citizens' desires to create more human bodies to add to society, teachers' desires reproduce society as a whole, allowing the achievements of the past to be conserved in the future.

Given the ideological investments that society makes in teachers as reproductive agents with a duty to the public, it should come as no surprise that communities have traditionally monitored and set limits on teachers' expressions of their own sexuality, from nineteenth-century laws preventing teachers from taking part in courtship to more contemporary lawsuits concerning teachers' expressions of sexuality on social media. Nor should we be terribly surprised that any time repressive norms are established around any aspect of bodily pleasure, social fantasies arrive to accomplish a twofold task: allowing the public to both enjoy the transgressive thrill of subverting the norm while at the same time allowing us to judge the transgressive act that thrills us. As Edelman's (2004) study of queer identity in the public imaginary suggests, our judgments in these cases of perversity are not about any particular act or type of person but instead are an attempt to maintain and uphold an ideal of "reproductive futurism," (p. 2) in which every aspect of personal pleasure requires some attending sense of civic responsibility to serve as its fig leaf. From Edelman's perspective, teachers might be viewed as ideal prisms of reproductive futurism, incorporating in one image all of society's conservative anxieties about the future as well as a transgressive impulse to subvert the reproduction of the same.

When we look at the relationships played out between teachers and students in pedagogical drama dating back to Plato's *Symposium*, the transgressive impulse manifests itself as a pursuit of pleasures that flouts the sacred, civic duty of education as future-oriented cultural reproduction by breaking with the social norms that schools are designed to promote. In reading or watching the stories of Martha, Blanche, Hector and many other literary teachers, we are morally torn between the characters' failures to uphold their social function and the fact that their transgressions give expression to a humanity that remains inexpressible within the discourses that constitute their role in the social order.

Our fascination with both real and fictional accounts of transgressive teachers demonstrates our investment in questions about how, and to what extent, our social and educational environments shape us. If teachers were no more than ideals of adult health, perfectly formed by the standards of society, we might have cause to be concerned that our own beliefs, ideals and desires might be no more than functions of a social order in which our individuality is erased. But Wilson's chapter shows us how teaching itself can serve as an ideal example of our basic, human refusal to be whatever is best or most useful for society. The characters may be fulfilling their social functions as teachers, preparing students to meet the world, but at the same time they stand out as exceptions and perversions, their desires impervious to the normalizing force of their social environments.

Contrary to the procreative, future-oriented standards that are often upheld in educational discourses, the sexual deviancy of fictional teachers tells us that the purpose of life is not more life nor is it a tinkering toward a perfected civilization through multiple generational drafts. Instead, these narratives of transgressive teachers seem to be showing us that the purpose of life is to enjoy it with a kind of joy that is not reducible to social approbation or the expectation of some future reward. Teaching and learning and the fragile, human connections that happen in those activities *are* the rewards, as simultaneously trite and terrifying as that may seem. Even in narratives where we cannot morally support the specific transgressions that fictional teachers commit in their pursuit of unsanctioned pleasure, we can still recognize their refusal to be no more than a function of social reproduction as a site where the possibility of being human, of being flawed, and of enjoying difference might be held open.

References

Bauer, D. M. (1998). Indecent proposals: Teachers in the movies. *College English, 60*(3), 301–317.

Chennault, R. (2006). *Hollywood films about schools: Where race, politics, and education intersect.* New York: Palgrave.

Dalton, M. (1999). *The Hollywood curriculum: Teachers and teaching in the movies.* New York: Peter Lang.

Dewey, J. (1944). *Democracy and education.* New York: The Free Press.

Edelman, L. (2004). *No future: Queer theory and the death drive.* Durham, NC: Duke University Press, 2004.

Farber, P., Provenzo, E., & Holm, G. (Eds.). (1994). *Schooling in the light of popular culture.* Albany: State University of New York Press.

Stillwaggon, J., & Jelinek, D. (2016). *Filmed school: Desire, transgression and the filmic fantasy of pedagogy.* London: Routledge.

2   Educating Frank
Mentorship in Willy Russell's *Educating Rita*

Richard Corley

In Willy Russell's popular 1980 play, *Educating Rita*, a student returns to thank her professor for his mentorship, offering him this assurance: "You think you gave me nothing, did nothing for me...but I had a choice. I chose, me...Because of what you'd given me. I had a choice. I wanted to come back an' tell y'that. That y' a good teacher" (Russell, 2007, p. 80). But what makes him a good mentor? What is the line between mentorship and friendship? At what period should mentorship end, and what should replace it? What issues related to gender and power are exposed through the mentorship process? Russell offers a lens through which to answer these questions when assessing the behavior of Frank, the play's mentor, and his work with Rita, his student. In the following chapter, I examine mentorship in the context of teaching and explore the mentorship depicted in the play, drawing on two productions of *Educating Rita* which I directed: the first in 2007 at the Berkshire Theatre Festival and the second in 2011 at Shattered Globe Theatre in Chicago.

Willy Russell's *Educating Rita*

Set in the north of England (ostensibly Russell's hometown of Liverpool), *Educating Rita* tells the story of Rita, a 26-year-old hairdresser who signs up for a course at the Open University (OU). The OU, founded by the 1960s Labour Party, was originally conceived to be a free "university of the air," which would broadcast television and radio classes for stay-at-home mothers and workingmen in order to raise the general level of education and develop a greater number of scientists and engineers for Britain. At the time of *Educating Rita*'s premiere (1980), there were roughly 70,000 students taking OU courses (Russell, 2007).

Rita's tutor, Frank, a shambling professor in his early 50s who'd rather be in the pub, takes on Rita as a pupil to earn some extra cash. Over the course of a year, with Frank's support, Rita's education leads her to question her working-class life. She leaves her husband, travels and decides to step into an unknown future of, for the first time, her own choosing. At the same time, Frank's staid existence is shaken by Rita's youth, curiosity and courage, and his life is upended.

Educating Rita, commissioned by the Royal Shakespeare Company, opened in London in June of 1980, starring Julie Walters and Mark Kingston, directed by Mike Ockrent; it subsequently ran for three years in the West End. Today, the play continues to be performed around the world and is on the syllabus of the General Certificate of Secondary Education (GCSE) Key Stage 4 (equivalent to American high school) in the United Kingdom.

One reason for the play's popularity is its variation on the popular Pygmalion and Galatea myth, recounted in Book X of Ovid's *Metamorphoses*, which tells the story of the sculptor Pygmalion and his creation, a statue of a woman that he longs to bring to life. When his wish is granted by Aphrodite, he and his creation marry. Pygmalion and Galatea have been the source of many works of visual and performing art, including paintings by Gerome, Shaw's play *Pygmalion,* and ballets and operas by Rameau, Eifman and Donizetti. It has echoes in Shakespeare's *The Winter's Tale,* in which a statue of Queen Hermione is brought to life at the play's end, and in the comic book character Wonder Woman, who is sculpted from clay by her mother Hyppolyta and given the breath of life by Aphrodite (Marston, 1942). What these stories have in common is that a woman attains full cognizance under the energizing gaze of a man. In the current era of redefined gender dynamics, the Pygmalion and Galatea myth carries a great deal of baggage. In a recent *New York Times* review of a production of Shaw's play, Soloski (2018) described the myth this way: "Boy meets rock. Boy carves rock into a girl. Boy pervs on girl. Boy gets girl…a grotesque comedy."

Mentorship

In a 2012 article, Cohen considered the relationship between teachers and mentors: "A teacher has greater knowledge than a student; a mentor has greater perspective. In this sense, a mentor is more like an editor—or the best kind of editor" (para. 1). She compares

Maxwell Perkins, who helped Thomas Wolfe clear away the clutter in his writing to reveal his true author's voice, to Gordon Lish, who may have imposed his own vision on Raymond Carver's work. She also considers her father's editorship of her writing as a young girl, in which he

> imposed his own voice and inserted his own predilections into my work when I was too young to have my own. Hence, he helped to shape these things in me while also delaying and possibly inhibiting the development of my own style.
>
> (para. 2)

And to that of her husband and a colleague, who "helped me clear away the clutter that obscured what I wanted to say. They listened to and nurtured my voice" (para. 3).

One of the implied insights by Cohen (2012) is that mentorship takes place over time and involves a commitment to the student's maturation through time. In a 1983 study, Kram identifies four common ways that a positive mentoring relationship develops over time:

> an *initiation* phase, during which time the relationship is started; a *cultivation* phase, during which time the range of functions implied expands to maximum; a *separation* phase, during which time the established nature of the relationship is substantially altered by structural changes in the organizational context and/or by psychological changes within one or both of the individuals; and a *redefinition* phase, during which time the relationship evolves a new form that is significantly different from the past, or the relationship ends entirely.
>
> (p. 614)

Kram's (1983) definition of mentorship phases provides insight into the core competencies of good mentorship, reflected in Johnson's (2015) Triangular Model of Mentor Competence, which is based on "the presence of foundational character virtues (integrity, caring, prudence), salient foundational abilities (cognitive, emotional, relational), and numerous skill-based competencies (e.g., providing support, respecting autonomy, allowing increasing mutability)" (pp. 60–61). The triangular structure of Johnson's model suggests that it is not the individual elements that are paramount; instead it is the "integration of the virtues, abilities, and competencies in relationship with students...that characterize genuine competence in the mentor role" (p. 61).

Significantly, Johnson (2015) mentions cognitive ability as only one of nine elements of mentor competence. In other words, possessing superior knowledge isn't the primary factor in mentorship, but one of many. Referring to recent studies of successful mentoring, he determines that "ultimately, it was the mentor's interpersonal skill (vs. instructional talent) that served to most powerfully bond the student with the professor" (pp. 116–117). As noted above, one of Johnson's "foundational virtues" of mentoring is caring, or empathy, which "is most directly expressed through active and deliberate listening" (p. 117).

Johnson's (2015) perspective is seconded by Ken Bain (2004) is his popular recent book *What the Best College Teachers Do*. Though Bain focuses on aspects of good teaching, his observations can be applied productively to mentoring:

> If you ask many academics how they define teaching, they will often talk about "transmitting" knowledge, as if teaching *is* telling. That's a comforting way of thinking about it because it leaves us completely in control; if we tell them, we've taught them. To benefit from what the best teachers do, however, we must embrace a different model, one in which teaching occurs only when learning takes place.
>
> (p. 171)

The best mentorship practices, then, involve interpersonal transactions in which the mentee's success is the result of the mentor's emotional intelligence and instinct. As Salerni (personal communication, 2018) explains,

> Mentoring is empathy in action. It is asking the probing questions that help a mentee clarify what s(he) is struggling to articulate. Mentoring is entering into and trying to maintain an intimate creative partnership with the mentee under your supportive wing for such a short time.

In summary, quality mentorship is *empathetic* (a good mentor imagines him/herself in the personal experience of the student), *respectful* (a good mentor respects him/herself, the student and the relationship mutually created between the two), *integrative* (a good mentor is concerned with assimilating students' learning and life experiences in order to create wholeness, change and transformation) and *creative* (a good mentor allows for improvisation, rather than adhering to a formula). To return to Cohen's (2012) key descriptor, these qualities give the mentor the kind of perspective that allows the mentee's voice to emerge.

Initiation in *Educating Rita*

During the initiation phase of his mentorship, Frank displays little empathy. As he prepares to meet his new charge, he takes a call from Julia, his partner, and says that he won't be home for dinner. "I've got this Open University woman coming this evening, haven't I?" he tells her, adding that

> I shall no doubt *need* to go to the pub afterwards if only to mercifully wash away some silly woman's attempts to get into the mind of Henry James or Thomas Hardy or whoever the hell it is we're supposed to study on this course.
> (Russell, 2007, p. 1)

Later, near the end of the first scene, he will try to get out of teaching Rita by telling her, "I'm really rather an appalling teacher… most of the time that doesn't matter…most of my students are themselves fairly appalling. And the others manage to get by despite me" (p. 15).

Frank's disdainful view of education has been shaped by his experience teaching in a fact-based system in which self-knowledge has no place; his work is the kind of one-way knowledge transmittal decried by Bain (2004). "Everything I know – and you must listen to this –," he tells Rita, "is that I know absolutely nothing" (Russell, 2007, p. 15). For Frank, the view of education that permeates the English system does little to help students' creative imaginations and may stifle them: "We pluck birds from the sky and nail them down to learn how they fly" (p. 26).

As quoted in Bain (2004), de Beaugrande viewed this as bulimic education, which "force-feeds the learner with a feast of 'facts' which are to be memorized and used for certain narrowly defined tasks, each leading to a single 'right answer,' already decided by teacher or textbook" (p. 41). This kind of education turns students into fact-bingers and purgers, robotically doing what they can to survive in the memorization culture of the system. It takes advantage of the mind's exceptional ability to program and retain meaningless information but leaves out the further step of placing "memories and experience into a 'whole'...which tells us how things in space relate and how ideas and experiences are connected" (Caine & Caine, 1997, p. 18). Instead of force-feeding Rita facts, Frank will attempt to promote wholeness by helping her connect her autobiography to her earning.

Cultivation in *Educating Rita*

As their relationship moves to the cultivation stage – the major part of the play – one of Frank's remarkable aspects is how deeply he listens to Rita and how many questions he asks her about her life. He possesses the first quality of good mentorship: empathy. Russell ignores the typical "boundary setting" of mentor/mentee relationships by having Frank drink during their sessions and Rita veer away from her lessons to share intimate details of her personal life. However, in blurring the relationship, Russell dramatizes Salerni's (2018) concept of "empathy in action" and shows that a teacher must be open to responding to a student's needs, above and beyond the subject at hand. When Rita opens up to Frank about her marriage, and asks him about his divorce, Frank recognizes that she is looking for perspective and perhaps validation in her discomfort at home.

In the cultivation phase, Frank begins to show Rita a great deal of respect. He curtails his drinking; he works harder; he disciplines himself and demands that Rita discipline herself – that she be on time and more rigorous and hard-working in her studies. He tells her,

> Now you listen to me! You want to learn, and you want me to teach you. Well, that, I'm afraid, means a lot of work, for you as well as me...Possessing a hungry mind is not in itself a guarantee of any kind of success.
>
> (Russell, 2007, p. 27)

Respect, in this regard, means demanding more from the student than she might believe she is capable of accomplishing. However, there is another kind of respect that Frank shows Rita, which helps to create what Johnson (2015) calls a fiduciary relationship, in which trust is established between mentor and mentee. By taking Rita to a play, inviting her to have a home-cooked dinner with Julia and his friends and sharing many details of his life, Frank shows that he trusts Rita and invites Rita to trust him with the circumstances of her life beyond school.

Perhaps the most striking aspect of Frank's mentorship of Rita during the cultivation phase is the way he asks her to see the meaning of literature in the context of her life. When she shares her thoughts about the people she grew up with – "the meanin's all gone; they've got nothin' to believe in…everyone's caught up in the 'Got-to-Have game…'" (Russell, 2007, p. 33) – Frank brings her back round to her assigned reading of E. M. Forster by helping her see the link between her mates, her family and the characters in *Howard's End:*

FRANK: 'Only connect'!
RITA: Oh, not friggin' Forster again!
FRANK: 'Only connect' – you see what you've been doing?
RITA: Just tellin' y' about home.
FRANK: Yes, and connecting: your dresses/society at large/consumerism; drugs and addiction/you and your husband–connecting.
RITA: Oh.
FRANK: You see?
RITA: An' … an' in that book…no one does connect.
FRANK: Yes! Irony.

(Russell, 2007, p. 34)

By leading Rita toward integrative knowledge – connecting her learning to her life – Frank demonstrates a core function of mentorship: giving the mentee the tools to change. Once Rita sees her life in the context of other's lives, she has a more holistic understanding of her situation: she sees that she is not alone. This recognition of kinship is the first step toward her transformation; when she can imagine herself as being like the wider world, she is able to imagine joining it. Frank's mentorship enables Rita's transformation, and in doing so, he shows himself to be a mentor who has perspective and a holistic view that "sees human beings as active, dynamic, self-organizing systems with a mind or a self capable of self-reflection, continuous growth, and change" (Johnson, 2015, p. 64).

By connecting himself to the off-campus world, and showing that connection to Rita, Frank displays what Johnson (2015) calls relational identity, a highly meaningful action defined as a mentor's ability to see oneself in relation to others. Frank's relational identity leads to reciprocity, in which the mentor, by connecting his world to the mentee, encourages the mentee to do the same. At the end of Act One, when Rita leaves her husband and shows up in his office with her suitcase, Frank has become more than her mentor: he is now her friend.

Separation in *Educating Rita*

Act Two of *Educating Rita* is almost wholly concerned with the separation phase, except for the play's final scene, where Frank and Rita briefly reassess their work together. Frank's work with Rita during the separation phase displays the dangers and challenges of mentorship. He tells her that if she continues with him, "to pass examinations, you're going to have to suppress...perhaps even abandon your uniqueness. I'm going to have to change you" (Russell, 2007, p. 52). What Frank is referring to is forcing her to conform to the university student model, one whose head is full of the facts and theories of others. In sculpting the raw clay of Rita into this kind of fact-consumer, Frank understands he may end up creating Frankenstein's monster and, in fact, his fears turn out to be warranted. Near the end of the play, analyzing his own poetry, Rita gives Frank the kind of rote, upper-level undergraduate opinion he warned her against: "You can see in it a direct line through to nineteenth-century traditions of – of like wit an' classical allusion" (Russell, 2007, p. 75). In response, he tells her that "like you I shall change my name: from now on I shall insist upon being known as Mary, Mary Shelley" (p. 76).

Cultivation doesn't always produce the kind of student for which a mentor hopes, which can lead to strain in the separation phase. Frank's mentorship of Rita has given her the freedom to choose a new set of values; in doing so, she has transformed herself into exactly the thing he was afraid of: an academic, spouting the party-line of her textbooks. What Frank doesn't see is that, for working-class Rita, her studies are a kind of crowbar prying open the door of her stifling marriage and neighborhood. Instead, Frank furiously denounces Rita's change: "Found a culture, have you, Rita? Found a better song to sing, have you? No – you've found a different song, that's all – and on your lips it's shrill and hollow and tuneless. Oh, Rita, Rita..." (Russell, 2007, p. 77).

For Frank, Act Two is dominated by emotions that, according to Kram (1983), characterize the separation phase: "turmoil, anxiety, and feelings of loss" (p. 618). Rita has started to outgrow Frank:

"What's up, Frank, don't y' like me now that...y' can no longer bounce me on Daddy's knee an' watch me stare back in wide-eyed wonder at everything he has to say?" (Russell, 2007, p. 77). She has grown in ways he did not expect and that he doesn't admire. She chafes at his expectations for her and at the power he holds over her, echoing the famous last line of Shaw's 'Sequel to *Pygmalion: What Happened After*': "Galatea never does quite like Pygmalion: his relation to her is too godlike to be altogether agreeable" (Shaw, 1916, para. 24). The modality of sculpting a living being is never uncomplicated or emotionally clean.

Redefinition in *Educating Rita*

The ending of *Educating Rita* demonstrates how Frank and Rita struggle to redefine the mentor/mentee relationship. In the play's final scene, Frank's life has hit its nadir: his drinking has cost him his job, Julia has left him for good and he is packing his office to move to a teaching post in Australia. He has no interest in redefining the relationship; in fact, he is annoyed when Rita shows up at his office.

It is Rita who actively redefines their relationship. First, she shares her feelings of gratitude: "I came to tell you you're a good teacher" (Russell, 2007, p. 79). More importantly, she acknowledges that Frank has been more than a mentor, more than a teacher to her, by telling him, "...I had a choice. Because of what you'd given me. I had a choice" (p. 79). Notice the echoes here to Cohen's (2012) tribute to those who helped clear away the clutter that obscured what she wanted to say. Because Frank nurtured Rita's voice, she can now redefine herself as separate from him and an agent of her own change.

Frank reciprocates by giving Rita a gift: a low-cut dress. It's not the kind of gift to create a clean break in the mentor/mentee relationship and redefine them as colleagues but Rita smartly counters it with an offer of her own: to cut Frank's hair. And so, the play ends, with Rita the former hairdresser reverting to doing what she used to do with her female clients: "See, most of them, that's why they come to the hairdresser's – because they want to be changed. But if you wanna change y'have to do it from the inside, don't y?" (Russell, 2007, p. 13). In this case, the gesture is loaded with meaning: "I'll change your outside," Rita seems to be saying to Frank, "the inside is up to you."

Educating Rita Today

In 1980, when Russell's play was first performed, audiences were primed to view it through the lens of its performance tradition: the Pygmalion/Galatea myth, yet another story of a man refashioning a woman in his image. An audience today is likely to reframe the story, taking note of the quasi-abusive methods used by Frank to shape Rita, or more significantly, the way that Rita, by refusing Frank's attempts to sculpt her, interrupts a pedagogy based on patriarchal notions of the unformed woman. In the era of troubling revelations of male abuse of power, in higher education and elsewhere, it is no longer possible to see Frank's mentorship of Rita as benign, but current audiences might consider how Rita's resistance educates and transforms Frank, making him a better teacher and mentor as well as a man who is more enlightened in his relationships with women.

While Frank's mentoring of Rita exhibits negative qualities – he drinks; he pushes boundaries; he aggressively derides some of her choices; he has a hard time letting her go – he also possesses many of the merits identified by Johnson (2015), Bain (2004) and Salerni (2018). He is deeply empathetic, he encourages integration, and, in the end, he respects Rita for who she is. He creates a fiduciary relationship with her by entrusting her with his life and becoming her friend. Under his guidance, Rita is transformed from a hungry person of limited vision to a dynamic, creative, empowered person with insight and discernment. She gives Frank a great deal of credit for the change in her, which manifests itself most profoundly in her newly acquired ability to choose her destiny. In the play's final moments, when Frank asks her what she will do next, Rita responds, "I dunno. I might go to France. I might go to me Mother's. I might even have a baby. I dunno. I'll make a decision, I'll choose. I dunno" (Russell, 2007, p. 81). In the final analysis, Frank gives Rita perhaps the most important gift a mentor can give a mentee: the ability to see her life as open to possibility and to know she has the freedom to shape it herself.

I have directed *Educating Rita* twice. The first time, I had yet to begin my teaching career. As the father of young daughters, I saw the play primarily as the story of a woman's search for self. I charted the progress of Rita's journey through the play, from hungry mind to willful individual, and supported her triumphant growth at every turn. The second time, I was influenced by two things: the way my now teenaged daughters had taught me to listen more and create a safe space for them to become women, and the way my teaching career at the University of Illinois-Chicago was revealing the challenges of working with students from low-income households. I shifted my point of view to one that was less triumphal and more transactional: It became a story not only about a woman's growth but one of questions about education itself, its efficacy and its outcomes. This production was greatly enhanced by the casting of a Black woman, Whitney White, as Rita, a casting choice that reframed the play in contemporary power politics: Rita was not only struggling to be accepted into the academic world, she was also attempting to become a part of the prevailing White culture. Questions surrounding Black upward-mobility and assimilation were essential to *Educating Rita* in my second production, and, to its credit, the play sustained those new questions, proving its continued relevance.

References

Bain, K. (2004). *What the best college teachers do*. Boston, MA: Harvard University Press.

Caine, R. N., & Caine, G. (1997). *Education on the edge of possibility*. Alexandria, VA: ASCD.

Cohen, P. M. (July 24, 2012). Teaching vs. mentoring. *The American Scholar*. Retrieved from https://theamericanscholar.org/teaching-vs-mentoring/#.XAsxRBNKifU

Johnson, W. B. (2015). *On being a mentor: A guide for higher education faculty*. New York: Routledge.

Kram, K. E. (1983). Phases of the mentor relationship. *Academy of Management Journal*, 26(4), 608–625.

Marston, W. M. (1942). *Wonder Woman #1*. New York: DC Comics.

Russell, W. (2007). *Educating Rita*. London: Methuen Student Editions, Bloomsbury.

Shaw, G. B. (1916). *Pygmalion*. In *Sequel: What happened afterwards*. Retrieved from https://www.bartleby.com/138/6.html

Soloski, A. (March 27, 2018). Review: A playful 'Pygmalion' from Bedlam? Bloody likely. *New York Times*. Retrieved from https://www.nytimes.com/2018/03/27/theater/pygmalion-review-bedlam-theater.html

Response to Chapter 2
Educating Rita Today

Andrew Goodwyn

In responding to this chapter, I read Willy Russell's (2014) very latest version of the play, which he has carefully adjusted to remove the specific contemporary references that were in the original text. In doing this, he says in his author's note to the revised edition that he wanted to make the play "be perceived as taking place in its own time" (p. v) and not anchored in the attitudes of the late 1970s/early 1980s. He also makes it clear that this is not because the play is often studied in educational contexts and that therefore teachers and students are his priority; his main consideration "is with the companies that act my plays and the audiences that watch them" (p. v).

This principle is an excellent one. The idea of studying plays as a set of fixed words on a page is something that still negatively dominates far too much teaching in high school classrooms in particular. Probably Shakespeare suffers most, so often being taught as a dramatic poem rather than as a text to be sounded out and acted out. This version of Russell's rightly famous and enduring story is given a longer lease of life through its author's willingness to float it free of the prescriptions of dates.

Corley's exploration of the play has a similar spirit, concentrating on the universalist elements of the mentor to mentee relationship, dramatized by gender, class and – initially – education. This is a serious theme for any teacher to explore with a class in almost any school in the English-speaking world, where all these factors are current, not in a distant past. The play at its simplest plot level is about an experienced university tutor inducting a new student into the world of academic discourse. At the next plot level, it concerns a knowing male mentor guiding a novitiate female mentee through a difficult experience and a transformative life-changing opportunity. At the true dramatic level, it explores the improbable collision between a disillusioned and self-loathing but powerful gatekeeper and the young apprentice, full of naïve hope and aspiration: the energy transfers between them in both directions, both are permanently changed through their encounter, both become more truly 'educated'.

Before responding to the perspective of Corley and his own productions, we must not lose sight of the wonderful humor that infuses this dramatic experience. The marvelously entertaining moment when Frank reads out Rita's response to solving the staging problem of Ibsen's *Peer Gynt*, and reads "put it on the radio" (Russell, 2014, p. 31) is a sure laugh but with a fascinatingly multi-layered meaning. Firstly, she is absolutely right: that would solve the problems and she did not need an academic essay to prove her point. Secondly, Frank loves that response and for him it represents what he finds so fascinating about educating Rita: that she already has real knowledge and insight. Thirdly, at that stage in their relationship, he is still educating Frank; he knows she needs to acquire the trappings of academic discourse in order to pass those examinations and is genuinely puzzled as to how to approach being her tutor.

Fourthly, the names Frank and Rita matter. Rita is, in real life, actually named Susan, but chose 'Rita' to be different from family and community choices made for her. Frank, in the sense of honest, is not frank at all with himself; he finds his honesty in demystifying the games of academic success so Rita [authentically Susan and who later in the play reclaims her name] can go on to become her own person, partly through learning from Frank how to be, as he sees it later, a kind of academic ventriloquist but, for her, a woman who has found her voice. Later, Frank is so horrified at his 'success' that he references Mary Shelley's *Frankenstein* with the implication that Rita is his version of the monster. And here we have another fantastic way to explore the play as a kind of literary palimpsest.

Willy Russell found his own voice through education. In the Modern Classics text autobiography (2009), Russell recounts his own move from hairdresser to famous playwright – perhaps *Educating Rita* is very much about educating Willy – and he recalls the moment in his early 20s when he first entered his local college and "felt at home" (p. 75). One home for him has been the educated world suffused with literature, where just mentioning Mary Shelley's *Frankenstein* – not the Frankenstein of popular culture but the classic of gothic literature from "unpopular" culture – puts the referent into that elite club of literary snobbishness.

For any teacher of English, the play is delightfully full of references and jokes that endlessly pun on writer's names, on famous titles and phrases such as 'only connect'. This is part of the play's rich ironic texture: that to get the jokes, you have to be like Frank, a man of letters; for them to be funny, you have to understand Rita's lack of knowledge. Russell is careful to invest Rita with a natural wit and sense of humor; she is confident enough to mock Frank and to make lewd and funny comments such as what exactly happens to Howards' appendage if it is an 'end'.

Frank is 'at home' amongst all these literary allusions but he has lost his way at the beginning of the play. His book-lined study hides whisky bottles as well as his deep sense of self-loathing, his 'failure' as a minor poet, his wish to 'buggar the bursar' and somehow find a way home – without going to the pub. Rita is his savior. Although she begins herself as someone who cannot find happiness in what she feels is her shallow, working-class culture, her freshness and profound desire to renew herself give Frank a chance for redemption – all be it in Australia.

Russell provides the teacher with this wonderful twist on the Pygmalion myth. Partly created by Frank, Rita is the statue that comes to life, that learns to speak a new language, just like Eliza Doolittle in Shaw's imagining, but she also escapes patriarchy and the narrow expectations of the stereotypical female roles that men like her husband would use to imprison her. In this version of the story, Frank [remember *Frank*enstein] is actually the monster as much as the creator. His drunken, at times boorish, behavior and complete disregard for his academic institution, his colleagues and his female partner, make him comic and at times rather pathetic; he really needs someone to remold him and bring him to life.

Corley's emphasis on the mentoring theme of the play focuses closely on the nature of developing other humans. Although Russell, in his new edition, has striven for the play to exist in its own dramatic time, nevertheless, there is a poignancy in the recognition of one major element of the context: the entitlement to an education that was represented by The Open University. Some high school students, who have the support of their family, will choose college straight away; some will go for employment, often because of both economic and familial pressures to get out and earn some money. The latter is what happened to Russell, aged 15. At the age of 18, Rita, because of her upbringing, deep disengagement with schooling and wish to fit with her peer group, would never have considered going to university. Rita is quite young – only 26 – and yet she already feels old; everyone expects her to have babies but she secretly takes birth control to preserve her slight independence from turning into her unhappy mother. Frank is 'old', a classic middle-aged man; he is to some extent a reluctant father figure.

Rita is not physically at university; she is on the kind of access or distance program that was pioneered by The Open University [OU] in the UK back in the 1960s for mature students who never had the aspiration for university at 18. This author was a mentor to many, mostly female, graduates from The OU who in later life were transformed and wanted to become teachers and transform the lives of others, and they certainly succeeded, becoming excellent teachers and role models and mentors themselves. Some of Russell's portrayal is true to life: Rita is studying part time, working on her reading and writing at home as best she can, supported by a tutor. It is also true to life that men resisted this in 'their' women, tore up their books, took the electric plug off the television to stop them accessing Open University programs, made them do their academic work in the freezing back room. The OU students, especially the female, mature students like Rita, went to summer schools for two weeks and were transformed by the experiences, often leading to marital breakdowns. Often these women achieved their degrees and then went on to successful careers, some, as mentioned above, to become teachers.

What is true to drama, but not life, is the play being set in Frank's study in a traditional university. Most such tutorials were held in bleak and empty school classrooms in the evenings or at a local college. But for the drama, Frank and Rita act out the mentor to mentee relationship, the Pygmalion and Frankenstein myths, in the holy shrine of academic life – the study – in the hallowed spaces of a proper university. Outside students loll on the grass and discuss the merits of *Lady Chatterley's Lover* and Rita, as she grows in confidence, becomes friendly with these young students; one young man offers a little seductive rivalry to 'old' Frank. But it is to Frank she stays true and returns, having passed the exams and finally written that essay on staging Ibsen. This is great drama and based on true life but, for the teacher, there is great potential in the classroom to consider Rita's struggle for personal freedom. Her desire to escape the limitations of her particular community, her wish to not become her mother who weeps with frustration, her liberation – all this comes through an education in literature, Frank's great gift to her forever. This play is not just about educating Rita, then; it is about the emancipatory power of education, especially for those who must struggle against inequalities and repression.

The play has a kind of happy ending. Frank, with his now neat hair, thanks to Rita's old skill set, can at least attempt redemption in a New World. Susan, having reclaimed her name and freed herself, now educated, can make her way in the Old World, but one still dominated by class and gender inequalities. Susan was never sentimental; she began her real education with a degree of necessary naivety. Her early illusion that being able to speak like Frank would change the world for her is replaced by a truer understanding that she has changed, and now she has choices. She thanks Frank because, although she is really not sure what to do – she might go to France, she might have a baby – as her teacher, he gave her help in reaching home, a place where she says "I chose me." For the teacher and the class, this play is a moving and funny experience, full of life, full of laughter, with plenty of pain and failure to keep it anchored in real life but with the profoundly optimistic message that education can set you free.

References

Russell, W. (2009). *Educating Rita* (Modern Classics). London: Bloomsbury Methuen Drama.

Russell, W. (2014). *Educating Rita*. London: Bloomsbury Methuen Drama.

3 *Fun Home*

Representations of a Fractured Father

Heather Welch

Kron and Tesori's 2014 musical *Fun Home,* based on Alison Bechdel's (2006) autobiographical graphic novel *Fun Home: A Family Tragicomic,* focuses on Alison's discovery and disclosure of her own sexuality. Within Alison's journey, the musical also presents the relationship with her father, Bruce, a complex man who is alternately portrayed as a demanding high school English teacher, a distant father and a closeted gay man who possibly committed suicide shortly after Alison told him that she was a lesbian. As Alison explores her childhood and adolescence and seeks to determine the authenticity of her memories about her family, she also considers the strong, albeit complicated, bonds that exist between father/daughter and teacher/student.

This chapter explores the representation of Bruce Bechdel in the musical *Fun Home,* one that blurs the lines between teacher and father. In many ways, Bruce is an intellectual and social guide to his daughter, intent on teaching her a wide range of things important to him: the beauty of art and literature, his beliefs of normative social cues and dress. These things are emphatically repeated to Alison throughout the musical, and, as younger versions of Alison resist his overbearing ways, it is through this posthumous exploration that Alison simultaneously realizes the complex duality between a man who so formatively shaped her identity and one whose inability to come to terms with his sexuality ultimately results in an inability to connect with his daughter as a father or a teacher when it matters most.

Bruce Bechdel As Parental Representation

Bruce's obsession with beauty and harmony is captured in one of the first scenes in the musical. Bruce has just retrieved items from an old barn that will be used to meticulously restore his large Gothic Revival Victorian home. As he separates the beautiful and the valuable from the "crap" (Kron & Tesori, 2014, p. 10), he is in his element, surrounded by beauty and harmony, discovering and exploring the depths and possibilities of his found treasures:

BRUCE: (Rapturously inspecting the wadded fabric.) No—
Linen
This is...linen
Gorgeous Irish linen
See how I can tell?
Right here, this floating thread, you see?

(Kron & Tesori, 2014, p. 10)

Bruce's efforts to construct a perfect physical world extend to the humans living in the house, as well. Under Bruce's artful hand, his wife, Helen and their three children, Alison, Christian and John, become ornamental artifice, a superficial representation of a beautiful family living in a beautiful house. The audience understands the superficial nature of this world, however, when the family prepares for someone to tour the house:

HELEN:
Kids? An important lady is on her way over here to see the house—Listen to me, please—This is one of those times you need to do what I say quickly and without any shenanigans.

(Kron & Tesori, 2014, p. 13)

In the subsequent song, Helen instructs the children on the level of perfection expected to ensure that Bruce is not angered or upset by anything out of place; they must work together so that Bruce does not "allow the demons to seize him" (Kron & Tesori, 2014, p. 16). The family's fear is palpable throughout the song, even as Bruce speaks to the imaginary Mrs. Bochner during the tour:

FAMILY. (perky but tense)

BRUCE.
... Oh yes, I've done all the work myself. That's how we're able to afford the place? No, no, historic restoration is an avocation, but that is very flattering. I teach English at Beech Creek High, and the Bechdel Funeral Home is our family business. So I'm also a funeral director.

What's he after?
What are we doing?
Right foot is tapping
That means he's stewing
Stay very still and
maybe we'll please him

Make one wrong move
and the demons will seize him

(Kron & Tesori, 2014, p. 16)

Bruce's desire for beauty and perfection extends to his professional life as a high school English teacher. An avid reader, he surrounds himself with the intellectual beauty of literature and poetry, further constructing a façade of precision, harmony and intellect. This perfectly constructed façade comes at a price: the overwhelming feeling that Bruce must suppress his own inner sexual desires to present as a perfect husband, father and teacher.

A glimpse of these suppressed desires comes in snapshots throughout the musical, both through bits of dialogue that reveal the depths of this suppression between Alison and her mother, as well as revelatory conversations that adult Alison remembers from past moments with her father. Among these acts of suppression are Bruce's use of his role as a high school teacher to engage in sexual encounters with students, using his intellect and poetry as an aphrodisiac. Alison later learns that her father hired former students to assist with the home renovation and other projects and would then have affairs with them.

In a scene to flesh out Bruce's sexual repression, the musical depicts the first time Bruce invites a former student, Roy, over to the house. Roy enters Bruce's library and comments on how much work has been done to the house since the Bechdels' have bought it. What follows is the first glimmer of flirtation between Bruce and Roy:

ROY: You must be in good shape, old man.
BRUCE:
> Not too bad if I say so myself
> I might still break a heart or two
> You'd be surprised at what a guy my age knows how to do
> **He brings the sherry to Roy.**
> Want it?
ROY: Yeah.
BRUCE: Unbutton your shirt.

(Kron & Tesori, 2014, p. 31)

Another example of the way that the musical depicts how Bruce's sexual repression overtakes, and ultimately upends, the harmony of the family is through Bruce's alcoholic seduction to solicit the attention of a current (and underage) student:

BRUCE: Hey, Mark. Is that you?
MARK: Oh. Hey, Mr. Bechdel.
BRUCE: You wanna lift?

MARK: I'm not going far.

BRUCE: I'm happy to give a you a ride. Let me move these groceries. Get in.

...Wanna beer?

(Kron & Tesori, 2014, p. 45)

In this section of the musical, the scenes shift swiftly to show how this severe lapse in judgment undermines the very level of physical and intellectual harmony and perfection that Bechdel demands of himself as he crosses the line of acceptable behavior as a high school teacher engaging sexually with a student. Further, this lapse of judgment has legal and familial repercussions. The representation of the perfect father becomes "fractured" in this scene as Bruce must face a difficult truth when asked why he is wearing a suit:

BRUCE: I have to see a psychiatrist.

SMALL ALISON: How come?

BRUCE: Because I do dome dangerous things. Because I'm bad. Not good like you.

ALISON: Actually, it's because you were arrested, Dad. On a charge of "furnishing a malt beverage to a minor," which I believe is what they call a euphemism.

(Kron & Tesori, 2014, p. 47)

As clear as adult Alison's view is on the matter, Small Alison is very confused by this cryptic exchange and must turn to her mother to explain. It is Helen who Alison turns to (both as a child and as an adult) to explain Bruce's peculiar behavior and outbursts, all of which appear to stem from his overwhelming feelings of sexual repression:

HELEN: The ...um... A judge said he had to go. It's been very... complicated. We thought we might have to move, and then...

SMALL ALISON: Move?? Where would we go??

HELEN: We don't have to move. The judge said your dad could— could—see someone instead. I can't explain it any better. You don't need to worry. Everything's going to be fine.

(Kron & Tesori, 2014, p. 47)

Bruce's demanding nature and high expectations are both desirable and undesirable qualities. They are desirable in the classroom, perhaps, but the way in which the lines blur when informing the social construction of his daughter becomes an element of concern. Bruce also forges strong bonds with his students and provides an environment in which students feels comfortable, which again is a good thing, but Bruce's use of this tactic to groom potential young lovers from his former students muddies the line of good teaching and sends his behavior spiraling into a dangerous (and ineffective) territory.

Bruce Bechdel As an Intellectual Guide

Bruce's meticulous control on the physical world of his surroundings is coupled with his desire to serve as a strong source of fatherly and intellectual guidance for Alison. The audience sees one example of this in a scene where Bruce instructs and shapes Small Alison's childish attempt to draw a picture of the state of Pennsylvania. Bruce's guidance means Alison must learn the "right way" to draw the picture; telling her that she will "ruin the picture," Bruce convinces Alison to let him take over and show her how to do it correctly:

HELEN: (Coming in from the other room.) Bruce, it doesn't matter. It's a drawing.

BRUCE: What do you mean it doesn't matter? She's taking it to school. She's showing it in class. You know what, never mind. You want to take a half-baked mess to school, you want to embarrass yourself like that it's fine with me. Do what you want.

SMALL ALISON: (Holding the drawing out to him.) No, I like the one you did, Daddy.

(Kron & Tesori, 2014, p. 44)

Adult Alison, looking back on this memory, recalls her father's method of drawing the map:

ALISON:

Make this part look rugged…
Mm mm
Allegheny Plateau
This dark shaded stripe bum bum bum is the front
Paint the long ridges and valleys below
Mm mm.

(Kron & Tesori, 2014, p. 44)

She then breaks free and draws her own version, ruminating that while her father's guidance guided her cartooning as a child, she shaped her craft as an adult into something uniquely hers. Interestingly, Bechdel has noted that her father's strict guidance and control of color directly influenced her focus on drawing cartoons devoid of color (Bellafante, 2006).

Bruce also serves as an intellectual guide for his daughter by cultivating her passion for literature and poetry. As her high school English teacher, he connects with his daughter through his love of poetry and literature. When she leaves home to attend Oberlin College, he continues his guidance from a distance through long conversations, letters and phone calls. During her visits home, Bruce sends literature back with Alison to read in addition to her college course work – something college-age Alison doesn't question until her girlfriend, Joan, does:

MEDIUM ALISON: Yeah. He sends me books. We talk about them.
JOAN: He sends you books to read on top of your schoolwork?
MEDIUM ALISON: Yeah.
JOAN: That's a little weird.
ALISON: (Realizing) Is that weird? That's really weird.
MEDIUM ALISON: Why?
JOAN: I don't know. Like, what books?
MEDIUM ALISON: Like…
JOAN: Colette??
MEDIUM ALISON: Yeah.

(Kron & Tesori, 2014, p. 34)

Bruce's role as a literature teacher never strikes Medium Alison as strange; she simply complies with her father's orders. It is only when Alison, as an adult, is replaying the memory that she realizes Joan's point: a father sending his daughter off to school with reading lists isn't typical. Moreover, Bruce is requiring Alison read Colette, an early twentieth-century lesbian novelist, surely not a typical suggestion from a father. This is another indication that the relationship that Bruce and Alison share is truly a unique one blurring the line between father and teacher. Bruce spends his time attempting to teach his daughter something that he feels she must learn, making many of their interactions throughout the musical a lecture, rather than allowing a deeper parental connection, something that Alison deeply desires.

Bruce Bechdel As a Social Guide

A substantial component of educational and parental efficacy is the expectation that teachers (as well as parents) provide strong examples of social and moral guidance. Gallarin and Alonso-Arbiol (2012) examine the prevalence of parent attachment and aggressiveness that occur through the course of child socialization. They clearly identify that parenting style, as well as familial socialization, is a key component in how family social dynamics occur.

Bruce is in a position to be a strong source of fatherly social guidance over Alison in multiple aspects of her life. In each instance, he clearly defines the roles that they should both assume: he is the elder, the expert, while she is the child who should follow his explicit instructions. The audience sees this when Bruce controls the way Alison dresses by choosing "appropriate" attire for her. In one scene, Alison resists wearing a dress that Bruce has picked out for her:

SMALL ALISON:
This dress makes me feel like a clown.
I hate it!
BRUCE: That's enough. We're late.
SMALL ALISON: You're wearing a girl color.
An eye blink of rage which he channels into ultra-calm rationality.
BRUCE: Every other girl at this party is going to be wearing her prettiest dress and you want to put on... What? What? Your jean jacket? Trousers? S'alright with me. You understand you'll be the only girl there not wearing a dress, right? Is that what you want? You want everyone talking about you behind your back? S'alright with me, change your clothes. Well? Go ahead. You gonna change?
SMALL ALISON:
Maybe not right now.
Maybe not right now

(Kron & Tesori, 2014, p. 37)

Bruce's use of guilt and anger to convince Small Alison to wear what he thinks she should wear is not an isolated incident. In another scene, Bruce expects Alison to pin her hair back with a barrette, although she prefers a haircut that requires less maintenance:

BRUCE: ...Hey. Where's your barrette?
Small Alison grudgingly pulls it out of her pocket.
Put it back in. It keeps the hair out your eyes.
SMALL ALISON: (*Under her breath as she puts it back in.*)
So would a crew cut.
BRUCE: If I see you without it again I'll wale you
(Kron & Tesori, 2014, p. 56)

Another element of fatherly expectation and social guidance occurs when Alison goes away to her first semester at Oberlin College. There, she makes the self-discovery that she is a lesbian and decides to write her parents to tell them. Bruce responds, also by letter, with a lecturing tone that blurs the line between teacher and father.

BRUCE: Your mother's pretty upset though – not surprisingly, I guess. But I'm of the opinion that everyone should experiment.
MEDIUM ALISON: (*Grossed-out.*) Seriously?
BRUCE: I can't say, though, that I see a point of putting a label on yourself. There have been a few times in my life that when I thought about taking a stand, but I'm not a hero. Is that a cop out? Maybe so. It's hard sometimes to tell what's really worth it.
(Kron & Tesori, 2014, p. 55)

Alison is angered by her father's response, a mix of parental guidance and societal instruction that attempts to come off as understanding while lacking acknowledgment and acceptance:

MEDIUM ALISON: The *tone* is what I can't stand. It's so typical. So all knowing. He has to be the expert. Lots of wisdom and advice about things he doesn't know anything about! I'm gay. Which means I'm not like him, and I've *never* been like him, and he can't deal with that.
(Kron & Tesori, 2014, p. 55)

Speaking to her mother, this time by telephone, offers more insight and Alison learns a long-held family secret:

HELEN	MEDIUM ALISON
...I don't like parents who meddle, but in this case I'm uniquely qualified to warn you against romanticizing this path. Alison, you probably don't know that on more than one occasion catastrophe has has been narrowly averted and it is difficult for me to—	Oh, please Catastrophe? Could you be a little more overdramatic?

HELEN: Alison, your father has had affairs with men. (*A beat.*)
MEDIUM ALISON: What?

(Kron & Tesori, 2014, p. 58)

When Alison returns home, she hopes to talk to Bruce about her sexuality, knowing now that he, too, is gay. She seeks solace and acceptance from her father, and a fleeting moment is offered on the last night of her visit when, while they are alone, Bruce briefly speaks of his earliest experience with a man:

BRUCE:
There was a boy
In college
My first year there
Norris Jones
He had black wavy hair

(Kron & Tesori, 1014, p. 69)

This is the last time they speak before Bruce's death, which is depicted in a final letter to Alison telling her all of the reasons he cannot live in the world anymore:

BRUCE:
...Who am I now? Where do I go?
I can't go back
I can't find my way through
I might still break a heart or two
But when the sunlight hits the parlor wall

> at certain times of day
> I see how fine this house could be
> I see it so damn clear
> Oh my God!
> Why am I standing here?
> **Glare of headlights. Unbearable deafening sound
> of car horn.
> And then he's gone.**
>
> (Kron & Tesori, 2014, p. 73)

Conclusion

Through the examination of her memories, Alison sets on a journey to discover what's true about her past as it is linked to her father and seeks to put into place the order of events that set into motion the elements of his – and therefore what is linked to Alison's – life. These distilled memories show that Bruce Bechdel served in the role of a teacher for Alison, often bypassing or blurring the lines of the parental role. By spending his time attempting to teach his daughter something that he feels she must learn, he does not allow a deeper parental connection, something that Alison deeply desires. Bruce's lessons clearly have a strong hand in the intellectual and social formation of young Alison. What ultimately becomes clear, however – and is the crux and conflict of the musical and these distilled memories – is that Bruce Bechdel's incapacity and inability to come to terms with his sexuality result in an inability to truly connect to Alison as a parent when she desperately needs and desires his fatherly advice the most.

In fact, the most cherished memory Alison holds of her father is a moment where they play the game "Airplane" that bookends the beginning and ending of the musical, highlighting that although their relationship was fraught with conflict, they held brief moments of perfection and these are the moments that she chooses to focus on:

ALISON:

> Caption: Every so often there was a rare moment of perfect balance when I soared above him
> **End**
>
> (Kron & Tesori, 2014, p. 73)

In sharing this final moment, the audience experiences the full journey of Alison's visceral investigation of her childhood, her father and herself. This captured essence of simple perfection provides an upbeat ending to a difficult subject of father and daughter struggles and self-identity It also provides a full-circle opportunity to see Alison and her father one last time, from the young girl's position of adoration for her beloved but fractured father.

References

Bechdel, A. (2006). *Fun home: A family tragicomic.* New York: Houghton Mifflin.

Bellafante, G. (2006, August 3). Twenty years later, the walls still talk. *The New York Times.* Retrieved from https://www.nytimes.com/

Gallarin, M., & Alonso-Arbiol, I. (2012). Parenting practices, parental attachment and aggressiveness in adolescence: A predictive model. *Journal of Adolescence, 35,* 1601–1610.

Kron, L., & Tesori, J. (2014). *Fun home.* New York: Samuel French.

Response to Chapter 3
The Complex Multiplicities of Teaching: Finding the Right Metaphor

Marshall George

In her chapter, Welch (2019) explores the blurred lines that create a complex duality for Bruce Bechdel, a father and English teacher in the musical *Fun Home* (developed from the graphic novel of the same name [2014]). Welch suggests that Bechdel, described as demanding and overbearing, has two identities: a fractured father and an intellectual guide. Bechdel believes that there is a right way to do things and does not rest until his daughter (and presumably his students) gets things right. Some might consider this notion of intellectual guide a good way to think about the role of teachers, and perhaps it does capture one aspect of teaching. However, teaching is far more complex than that. Just as we do not want to consider Bechdel a model teacher, intellectual though he may be, we also do not want to reduce teachers to guides on the side. Rather, teachers, both novice and experienced, should reflect on the complexities of teaching in order to articulate and understand the roles that they play as educators.

Educational philosophy scholars Biesta and Stengel (2016) have identified six iconic conceptions of the teacher that they suggest are "particularly influential in contemporary educational thought" (p. 13): Plato's dialogic questioner, Rousseau's responsive tutor, Dewey's democratic designer, Freire's liberator, Ranciere's critical egalitarian and Noddings' carer. They argue that, together, these conceptions of teachers' roles allow us to think deeply about teaching in paradoxical and complex ways. Lakof and Johnson (1980) made the case that creating metaphors for our everyday lives can help us to make deeper meaning of those lives. This is certainly true when contemplating the complexities of teachers' roles.

Considering Metaphors for Teaching

Years ago, I regularly taught a capstone course to teacher candidates in a secondary education program. In that course, the almost-graduates had to develop a portfolio aligned with the Interstate Teacher Assessment and Support Consortium (InTASC) Model Core Teaching Standards (Council of Chief State School Officers, 2013), identifying their teaching philosophies and showcasing their readiness to be professional educators. Citing the work of Lakoff and Johnson (1980), many of my students chose to identify a metaphor for teaching to organize their portfolio reflections and materials.

Over the years, I read student essays that cast the teacher as gardener, as artist, as navigator, as composer, as builder, among many others. Indeed, the work of a teacher often does take on characteristics of various other vocations and these roles and responsibilities certainly go well beyond the idea of teacher as an intellectual guide. My students' metaphorical conceptions of teaching offer insight into the complexities of teaching, especially from the perspective of novice teachers. As a reflective teacher educator, they caused me to wonder if we do enough to make teachers' multiple roles or identities visible to our preservice teachers. Do we provide them with opportunities to think metaphorically about the work of teaching? Do we sufficiently prepare them for the complex multiplicities of teaching?

In his chapter response, Rodesiler (2019) described the relationships between coaches and athletes and analyzed the power dynamics between the two. Reading his response, reflecting on the piece by Biesta and Stengel (2016) and revisiting Lakoff and Johnson (1980), I was reminded of the innumerable capstone portfolios I had read and considered what metaphor I would use to capture the complex multiplicities of teaching. In addition to being a professor in a School of Education, I also do a bit of consulting in New York City area schools, serving as an instructional coach to in-service teachers. Over the years, teachers have responded well to the concept of me being their coach as opposed to their supervisor or intellectual guide. Teachers may be served well to think of themselves as coaches when they are working with their students.

The Teacher Coach

I often have my preservice teachers read a short article by Carol Anne Tomlinson (2011) called "Every Teacher a Coach" in which she suggested, "Understanding the attributes of effective athletic coaches provides insight into the nature of good teachers and good teaching" (p. 92). But what are these attributes of effective athletic coaches? The Australian College of Physical Education (ACPE) has identified a list of qualities of effective coaches that mirrors those of effective, complex teachers, informing my own development of the teacher-coach metaphor. Stuart (n.d.), an ACPE blogger, identified leadership, knowledge of the sport, motivation, knowledge of the athlete and effective communication as the qualities of great coaches. Echoing the sentiments of Tomlinson (2011), I would argue that these qualities are equally important to think about when considering the complexities of effective teaching. Furthermore, I would argue that Bruce Bechdel does **not** demonstrate any of these qualities in *Fun Home*.

Leadership

According to Stuart (n.d.), "if the goal of great coaching is to guide, inspire, and empower an athlete or team to achieve their full potential, then that coach has to possess strong leadership qualities to accomplish these" (para. 2). The goal for great teaching is similar: great teachers must also be leaders in their classrooms as well as in their schools. Speaking to teachers, Spencer (2015) suggested,

> You may not think it, but the way you act, the characteristics you exert in class may have an influence on your students, so if you want your kids to grow up into great people and help lead another generation of children or students, make sure you are leading by example.
>
> (para. 3)

Indeed, teachers lead by example in their classrooms every day. For example, the way they interact with their students and colleagues should provide solid modeling for their students. Teachers should share their own reading, writing and other academic habits with their students, again leading by example. Simply by taking responsibility for their students' learning, teachers are engaged in an important leadership role. Likewise, when they collaborate with colleagues, parents and community members to meet the needs of their students, they are modeling good leadership. Bechdel's actions and interactions – with his students and, often, his family – would in no way be considered leadership by example.

Knowledge of Content and Pedagogy

Good football, basketball, baseball, lacrosse (or any sport) coaches need in-depth knowledge of the rules, the fundamental skills, offensive and defensive tactics and strategies for guiding and supporting the team during the game. Similarly, effective teachers need to have in-depth knowledge of the content that they are teaching. Shulman (1986) suggested, "To think properly about content knowledge requires going beyond knowledge of the facts or concepts of a domain. It requires understanding the structures of the subject matter" (p. 9). For example, English teachers need to know about the literary canon, the bourgeoning body of young adult literature, the structure and history of the English language, and the craft of composition and rhetoric (among many other aspects of English content). They do not need to have read every published work of literature but do need to know how to read any work of literature through a critical lens and how readers can respond to those works of literature that they read. Without this knowledge, an English teacher will struggle to be effective.

Bechdel knows and loves his content, as evidenced by his discussions with Alison, but he does not know how to engage her with that content in meaningful ways. He is an intellectual guide without any pedagogical moves. It is not enough for teachers to know and have passion for the content that they are teaching; they must also understand how to apply their knowledge of content to effectively engage learners in that content. Shulman (1986) referred to this as pedagogical content knowledge (PCK). He argued that PCK involves "an understanding of what makes the learning of specific topics easy or difficult: the conceptions and preconceptions that students of different ages and backgrounds bring with them to the learning of those most frequently taught topics and lessons" (p. 9). A teacher's knowledge and understanding of content and pedagogy is just as important as an athletic coach's knowledge of the game.

Motivation

Stuart (n.d.) stated that, "Coaches need to be able to convey passion to their players, to inspire them to get the most out of their performance" (para. 5). Likewise, passion and inspiration are key to successful teaching. As Tomlinson (2011) noted for teachers,

> The best coaches encourage young people to work hard, keep going when it would be easier to stop, risk making potentially painful errors, try again when they stumble, and learn to love the sport. Not a bad analogy for a dynamic classroom.
>
> (p. 92)

The best teachers do exactly the same thing.

The InTASC Model Core Teaching Standards indicate that a teacher must "understand the relationship between motivation and engagement and know how to design learning experiences using strategies that build learner self-direction and ownership of learning" (CCSSO, 2013, p. 21). This standard is supported by extensive research that confirms a positive association among student self-beliefs, academic motivation and academic outcomes (Capella, Aber, & Kim, 2016). While Bruce is passionate about literature, he is unable to inspire and motivate his daughter to feel the same. Alison follows her father's guidance but there is little evidence that she is inspired or motivated to learn on her own.

Knowledge of Learners

Athletic coaches need to know their players. They must know each athlete's strengths and areas in which they need to grow, as well as which players have synergy with each other, and build on those relationships for the good of the team. The same is true for classroom teachers. According to Hill and Chin (2018), "knowledge of students ranks high among teacher capabilities identified by both professional standards documents and scholars as important to good teaching" (p. 1066). The learner must always be at the heart of both teaching and coaching. But what does it mean for teachers to know their learners?

Teachers must understand that learners develop and learn differently and bring unique strengths and weaknesses to their learning. According to the InTASC standards (CCSSO, 2013), an effective teacher "understands how learning occurs—how learners construct knowledge, acquire skills, and develop disciplined thinking processes—and knows how to use instructional strategies that promote student learning" (p. 16). Teachers must not only have general knowledge of how their students develop and learn but also knowledge of the individual learners in their classrooms. Teachers must know about their students' interests, past experiences (academic and non-academic), personalities, academic strengths and areas where growth is needed. In a world with increasing diversity in our schools, teachers need to be effective in supporting students with a range of learning differences, bilingual and multilingual learners, academically gifted students and students at varying levels of readiness to learn.

Stuart (n.d.) suggested that coaches need to tailor their communication, means of motivation and approach to coaching to each individual athlete. Likewise, teachers who assume a coaching stance with their students need to understand and be willing to differentiate their instruction based on their knowledge of the learners in their classrooms. Bruce is in a unique position to understand his daughter as a learner but he makes little effort to do so; instead, he focuses on imparting his own interests to his daughter while ignoring her specific strengths and interests.

Effective Communication

While coaches/teachers sometimes work with the whole team/ class, they often also find it necessary to work with individuals or with small groups. In coaching their students, teachers must strive to encourage and motivate each student while helping them to develop the strategies and skills that will bring them success in their academic and real-world endeavors. To accomplish this, teachers must be able to communicate effectively with all of their students – orally, nonverbally and in writing. The description of effective communication skills for coaches presented in the ACPE blog sums up the same skills for teachers:

> An effective coach is able to set defined goals, express these goals and ideas clearly to players, give direct [actionable] feedback, reinforce key messages and acknowledge success. Listening is also a part of effective communication, so a coach should be a compassionate listener who welcomes player comment, questions and feedback.
>
> (Stuart n.d., para. 8)

Substitute the word teacher for coach, switch out player and student, and these words of wisdom are important for all teachers to hear. One of the most important aspects of teaching is clear communication of expectations, of instructions, of feedback. Unlike Bruce, who is not able to communicate meaningfully with his daughter, other students or his family, effective teachers must communicate effectively not only with their students but also with their families and caregivers.

In conclusion, no one metaphor accurately captures the complexities of teaching. Welch's identification of Bruce as an intellectual guide is reasonable but it is also problematic: not only is he not a good guide for his daughter and his students, but the metaphor does not capture the multiplicity of roles that a teacher should play. The metaphor of teacher as coach acknowledges the hard work, complex activities and necessary skills needed for effective teaching and can provide teachers, both novice and experienced, with an opportunity to reflect on the complexity of their work.

References

Biesta, G. J. J., & Stengel, B. S. (2016). Thinking philosophically about teaching. In D. H. Gitomer, & C. A. Bell (Eds.). *Handbook of research on teaching* (5th ed., pp. 7–68). Washington DC: AERA.

Capella, E., Aber, J. L., & Kim, H. Y. (2016). Teaching beyond achievement tests: Perspectives from developmental and educational science. In D. H. Gitomer, & C. A. Bell (Eds.). *Handbook of research on teaching* (5th ed., pp. 249–347). Washington DC: AERA.

Council of Chief State School Officers (CCSSO). (2013, April). *Interstate Teacher Assessment and Support Consortium (InTASC) Model core teaching standards and learning progressions for teachers 1.0: A resource for ongoing teacher development.* Washington, DC: Author.

Hill, H. C., & Chin, M. (2018). Connections between teachers' knowledge of students, instruction, and achievement outcomes. *American Educational Research Journal, 55*(5), 1076–1112.

Lakoff, G., & Johnson, M. (1980). *Metaphors to live by.* Chicago, IL: University of Chicago Press.

Shulman, L. S. (1986). Those who understand: Knowledge growth in teaching. *Educational Researcher, 15*(2), 4–14.

Spencer, B. (2015). The importance of leading by example. Retrieved from https://blog.teamsatchel.com/lead-by-example

Stuart, F. (n.d.). *Qualities of a great coach.* Retrieved from http://blog.acpe.edu.au/index.php/careers/qualities-great-coach/

Tomlinson, C. A. (2011). Every teacher a coach. *Educational Leadership, 69*(2), 92–93.

4 The Teacher's Ethos in William Mastrosimone's *Tamer of Horses*

Benny Sato Ambush

What does one do with a wild child when fate drops him into the lap of a middle-class suburban couple? Write him off and turn him into the authorities in a system that often chews up its wards rather than rehabilitates them? Take a chance on turning him around and risk getting mangled along the way? Does the answer differ if they are teachers?

This dilemma is one of the dramatic questions posed in William Mastrosimone's play *Tamer of Horses*, a gripping, emotional, often humorous, contemporary story about a teacher's need to get through to a character portrayed as an impossible bad seed. At the heart of the play is the personal ethos of teacher Ty Fletcher, the great lengths to which he, as a teacher, dares to go to reach a soul in trouble, the challenges he faces to his teacher's mission by corrupting influences, and the vital role that teachers – through Ty's representative example – play in our social fabric. The principles and attitudes of Ty Fletcher's personal ethos constitute the rudder that steers his moral conduct as a teacher, sometimes at great personal cost, for the sake of a higher goal.

I have directed *Tamer of Horses* three times, each time with cast members of color: Ty and Georgiane with Black actors and Hector with a Latinx actor. While race is not specified in the play, references in the text strongly suggest these characters are of color. In personal conversations, Mastrosimone himself confirmed that my hunches were accurate decades ago (personal communication, April 5, 2019). The dimensions that actors of color bring to these roles – and the consequent creation of teacher and student – broaden the play's resonance while maintaining its universality.

The Teacher Meets the Student

Ty Fletcher and his wife, Georgiane, teach at a private college prep high school in an American suburb. Although Georgiane grew up in the projects, her determination and grit, along with contributions from her sacrificing mother, earned her an education and entrance into the middle class. Ty and his brother, Sam, were orphaned at an early age after a fire killed both their parents. They were then separated in foster care. Ty's foster parents were teachers who planted in him the idea of service through education. Sam's circumstances offered no such guidance. As an adult, Sam was in and out of jail, as Ty explains to Georgiane: "When Sam got out the first time, he couldn't read. No skills. Unemployable. He fell between the cracks" (Mastrosimone, 2014, p. 51). Sam's subsequent violent death inspired Ty to choose his current life as an educator, a teacher of classic literature. Having resigned from his teaching position when pressured to artificially inflate grades, however, Ty now refurbishes antique furniture in his horse barn, his teaching put in hibernation.

Into their quiet life comes Hector St. Vincent, wounded from a barbed wire fence he scales in his escape from a youth house. Hector is an orphan, given up for adoption at birth by an unknown adolescent mother after a failed late-term abortion. He is hostile, wily, erratic, vulgar, violent, illiterate – and in need. While hiding out in the Fletchers' barn, Hector spooks the horses that Ty and Georgiane raise. When Ty investigates, the two meet, Hector with a homemade slapback knife and Ty with a pitchfork. With aggressive swagger, Hector reveals hints of his street gang life:

HECTOR: My shiv, man.
TY: When you go, you can have it back. Why do you have a shiv?
HECTOR: Why don't you have a shiv?
TY: I don't need a shiv where I live.
HECTOR: I need a shiv where I live.

(Mastrosimone, 2014, p. 6)

Ty recognizes a literal and spiritual hunger in Hector and wants to help him. Georgiane is skeptical when Ty chooses not to turn Hector into the authorities. Instead, Ty cuts a deal with him: Hector can stay in the barn in exchange for learning how to read. Ty operates on faith, believing that working with Hector is a worthwhile risk that could potentially turn Hector around.

Taming Hector

Although Hector cannot read, Ty senses an innate facility in him for imaginative poetic wordsmithing when he hears Hector rapping:

HECTOR

> Bob wire said
> "Your blood is red
> I wanna little taste
> You better jump back
> and here's a fact
> 'Cause you ain't gone no place."
> And then I said
> "Do your stuff,
> You ain't enough
> To keep me under control.
> Even wit a thousand teef
> Chew me up till I'm jus' roast beef.
> Bob wire!
> I'm changin' my address!
> Bob wire!
> You make a nasty mess!
> Bob wire! I really mus' confess
> I eat bob wire for breakfess!

(Mastrosimone, 1998, p. 24)

In his youthful bravado, Hector thinks he'll get rich as a famous rapper, be heard on the radio and perform in Madison Square Garden, with no need of a job or for reading: he'll hire someone to write down his raps if necessary. Ty tries to disavow him of that unrealistic and likely unattainable pipe dream by offering him something more substantial. Ty encourages Hector's verbal gift, though, telling him that "anybody who can have a conversation with barbed wire is a poet through and through. You have an ear for rhythm, an eye for imagery. You have a quick mind. And you have a bold musicality and exquisite sensitivity" (Mastrosimone, 1998, p. 35). He continues, however, by trying to teach Hector a larger lesson:

> That's why you wear a phony mask of tough guy – so that homes won't suspect how fragile you are. The Big Question is: Will the poet chuck the mask or will the mask be his face for the rest of his very short life?

(Mastrosimone, 1998, p. 35)

Ty explains to Georgiane that he sees potential in Hector:

> If I could spend a little time with him I might show him that he has powers greater than a slapback knife. He has a passion for words and poetry, for meter and rhyme, for wit. And he did it all on his own.
>
> (Mastrosimone, 2014, p. 51)

But Ty is also drawn to what Hector offers him: "What could he be if he had the right guidance?...In what little time we spent with him, something took...He sees something in me that makes him bare his soul" (Mastrosimone, 2014, p. 51). Ty is expressing his need as a teacher to sculpt and shape Hector's young life into a creative, contributing member of society and a fuller, more uplifted version of himself.

Ty uses his expertise in classic literature to form a deeper bond with Hector. Reading Homer's *The Iliad* aloud to Hector, Ty asks him to draw parallels to the Hector in Homer's ancient epic poem by recounting the essence of the story in his own words. The results are as profound as they are humorous and it is in this scene that Ty's teaching extends beyond imparting knowledge about great ancient literature: he is molding and shaping a human life in real time. Education for Ty is not requiring students to regurgitate facts, figures and information but, rather, to connect the wisdom in classic literature to the student's own life. Ty works with Hector where he is, drawing him out, engaging him fully, leading him to critically think about his life. Ty wants to put him on the road toward developing social and emotional intelligence, civic mindedness, ethical responsibility, and capacity to contribute productively to society – this is why he teaches. And, as he and Hector work in the barn, he can do this in ways that were hard to come by in his former school setting.

The Iliad, as one of the oldest extant works of Western literature, would be a bedrock text for Ty's classics class. Its warrior culture, heroes, themes of rage and hubris, love triangles and contentious clashes between rival factions is not just a compelling story, but also one familiar to Hector's street gang world. That a central figure in *The Iliad* bears the name Hector – a King's son and the greatest Trojan fighter – is a fortuitous point of connection that appeals to Hector's youthful machismo and bravura. The ancient Greeks retold such tales as the basis of pedagogy. It makes sense that Ty would try to make a connection with Hector using material easily translatable on his terms that could then be extended into teachable moments.

Hector is by no means miraculously changed, although a crack of possibility appears when he tells Ty, "You talk that shit you put snakes in my head, man!" (Mastrosimone, 2014, p. 29). Ty leaps at this embryonic emergence. As a teacher, he lives for a sign of forward progress. The student may never turn around – the student may, as Hector does, mess up repeatedly and mess over Ty and Georgiane, destroying their trust – but Ty's investment is worth it to him. He hopes that, despite the odds, something will get through to Hector and stick.

The Teacher's Ethos

In Ty Fletcher's example, we see teachers as outer-directed, selfless in devoting their time, energy and expertise to grooming, nurturing and encouraging expansion and growth in their students. This value-laden altruism is the distinguishing dispositional characteristic informing their behavior, work ethic and principled probity. Ty's decisions demonstrate these attributes. He champions the belief that reaching a human soul in hard-to-reach places is, despite the risks, an act of unconditional generosity necessary for the fulfillment of a teacher's essential purpose and the salvation of a nation. Far from being a simple act of goodwill, Ty accepts the challenge of helping a "lost" adolescent as much for himself as for Hector. Pygmalion-like, Ty takes on Hector as his personal project, lured by the chance to fulfill, in makeshift fashion, what he is made for: teaching. He doesn't need to be confined to a formal classroom; his classroom will be wherever he meets a student in need.

Tamer of Horses champions Ty's ethos by demonstrating the integrity of the teacher in the face of compromising pressures, whether teaching difficult students or holding fast to beliefs. Mastrosimone's revisions of the play through the years have evolved Ty as a teacher holding fast to his principles. One such evolution is the reason Ty leaves his prep school position. In an April 10, 1998 script revision, the school's Headmaster wants Ty to give a passing grade to a student in Ty's notoriously rigorous classics class; the student's current grade is insufficient to gain Ivy League college acceptance. The student's father threatens to withhold his sizable annual endowment check to the school if his son's grade doesn't change.

The Headmaster's pressure to lower Ty's standards of excellence for financial gain is anathema to Ty's ethos. Ty's resolute hold on applying pedagogical excellence equally to all students reflects the incorruptible, albeit stubborn, rectitude and sense of fairness embodied in his teacher's ethos. Rigging unearned grades, motivated by financial bribes, robs the student of the learning that can only come through participatory effort. The student is thus cheated of the very point of education, a travesty counter to Ty's ethos as a teacher. A teacher who conspires in such deceit corrupts himself and the student. A student with such an unearned advantage who lands a seat in a desired college robs other students who legitimately earned their way in.

The cost of Ty's intransigence is high. A much-needed stable income is gone and, as a result, Georgiane feels pressured to delay having a child, even as her biological clock runs down. Ty's teacher ethos will not permit him to go against himself no matter the financially pragmatic advantages. Whether Ty's choice not to yield to unethical behavior is honorable or foolish, a surrender just isn't in him.

Ty in the Real World

The rewards of teaching often are not measured monetarily. Ty teaches Hector how to read in his barn without pay, attempting to make him realize his need to be literate. Ty applies literacy pedagogically to Hector's moral conduct to liberate him from a life of limits:

TY:

> You think you don't need to read? Can you read the men's room sign? Or do you have to have a little picture of a man on the door? You want to drive a car? You have to take a written test, and you have to read signs along the road. Words. How do you pick a fight? Hard words. How do you stop a fight? Words. On Valentine's day, what's your girl want from you more than chocolate and flowers? Sweet words. What hurts her feelings? Words. What makes her smile? Tender words. How do you get married? Sacred words. How do you break up? Angry words.
>
> (Mastrosimone, 2014, p. 66)

The context of Ty's belief in Hector's need for literacy is born out in recent statistical data. As of 2018, more than 30 million adults in the United States cannot read, write or do basic math above a third-grade level (Room 241 Team, 2018). These low literacy rates costs the U.S. at least $225 billion each year through non-productivity in the workforce, crime and loss of tax revenue due to unemployment (National Council for Adult Learning, 2015). High school dropouts – likely possessing low rates of literacy – have a 7.7 percent rate of unemployment compared to high school grad-uates' rate of 5.3 percent (Bureau of Labor Statistics, 2017). Even if they are employed, those who lack proficiency in reading and writing will likely work in unskilled positions (Haynes, 2010) since 63 percent of all jobs will require at least some post-secondary education (Georgetown Center on Education and the Workforce, 2018). In fact, by 2020, it is estimated that 65 percent of all jobs – compared to 28 percent in 1973 – will require some form of post-secondary education (Georgetown Center on Education and the Workforce, 2018). The ramifications of low literacy rates extend beyond employment, however: Studies suggest that two-thirds of students who struggle with reading by fourth grade will run into trouble with the law at some point (Lake, 2016).

Ty recognizes that Hector is living in a world where literacy is an absolute precondition for success. By teaching Hector to read in his barn, he intends to plant and fertilize the seeds for Hector's poten-tial growth, open future employment prospects and ignite Hector's mind to better equip him for a successful, meaningful and produc-tive life. Ty believes that Hector's lack of literacy skills poses severe obstacles to him achieving a fruitful life – and the statistical data seem to support Ty's view. He believes his mission to shape, guide and transform Hector's literacy abilities and, by extension, his be-havior is the vital role the teacher plays in any society.

Mastrosimone's play, first written in the 1980s, also presciently addresses current trends in education that compromise the teacher's ethos, as Ty makes clear:

TY:
> But nowadays the classroom is geared up to mass produce great bellies with great appetites, to make more cogs for the machine. You want to prepare young minds for the world? Scrap philosophy. Teach them rhetoric. Teach them how to ar-gue to win. Scrap algebra, geometry and trig. Teach 'em how to cook the company books. Teach them insider trading. Scrap history. Rewrite it so it's more entertaining.
>
> (Mastrosimone, 2014, pp. 76–77)

The growing corporatization of American education runs counter to Ty's essential mission of teaching and serves interests other than the students. As Fontdevila and Verger (2019) state,

"A growing body of research points to the increased presence of private actors in education policy-making processes, frequently in connection with the advancement of a pro-market agenda...to reshape the education landscape...through a broad range of activities, including consulting, research, and evaluation...[that advocate] the desirability of including both private sector and for-profit motives in educational development strategies." (pp. 47–61)

Ty's ethical dilemma at his prep school – whether to pass an undeserving student – puts his teacher's ethos in an untenable crisis. It is also evidence of the very trends Fontdevila and Verger (2019) identify:

TY:

> At the end of the year I used to wait in my classroom for one student. The one I got to. One who would visit after exams and tell me the great epics gave him new eyes. Eyes that look down from the moon's surface and see the Earth and all the doings of mankind. But no student ever came to visit. I never got to one. My dad used to say: You teach 'em and they go and you hope they remember something.
>
> (Mastrosimone, 2014, p. 77)

Ty laments the abridging of student development by influences that pursue goals divergent from the blossoming of student potential. In stark relief is the value of his work with Hector in the barn, using a pedagogy he hopes can expand Hector's life possibilities.

The Origins of *Tamer of Horses*

During one of my early productions of *Tamer of Horses* decades ago, I phoned Mastrosimone and we discussed his reasons for writing the play. On April 5, 2019, he emailed me with further details about his inspirations and impulses for the play.

While a student in one of New Jersey's public high schools, Mastrosimone, by his own admission, was an undisciplined, unruly screw-up – a wild horse if you will. One day, a teacher dressed him down in the hallway, saying that he taught his brothers, that they were excellent students, so why was Mastrosiome a troublemaker and a class clown when he was obviously smart.

Embarrassed, Mastrosimone knew that the teacher, whom deep down he respected, had his best interests at heart. By calling him out on his behavior, Mastrosimone credits this teacher's intervention with helping him turn his life around. Mastrosimone told me that he wrote *Tamer of Horses* to express his thanks to the teacher who cared enough about him to stick his neck out to try to rescue him from himself.

Mastrosimone connects two of his past experiences directly to his creation of *Tamer of Horses*. First, he chose to make Ty a classics teacher because he studied *The Iliad* in prep school, which he attended after his public school experience, and again in college. He was deeply taken by the characters of Achilles, Patroclus, Paris and Hector, and he could see it all as an epic movie in his head.

Second, years later when he was on a train leaving Newark Penn Station, a gang of snatch-and-run kids got on the train, harassing and robbing people. He didn't see the robbery but heard people yell and scream. He stood up as the kids ran through the train, preparing to defend himself. Two kids ran past him as the train began to brake. One kid knew how to open a door and called to the other kid, "Hector, this way!" Hector went for the open door that his friend was holding just a few feet from Mastrosimone. He and Hector made eye contact, then, Hector was gone. Shortly thereafter, Mastrosimone connected the Hector on the train with *The Iliad*: "Here's a street dog named after a great hero – if only he knew" (personal communication, April 5, 2019). *Tamer of Horses* began in Mastrosimone's head as he carried on an imaginary conversation with the Hector on the train, telling him that his name comes from a great hero, just as Ty does with Hector in the play.

The Teacher Ethos

Mastrosimone's portrait of teacher Ty Fletcher in his play *Tamer of Horses* lives in the realm of what could (and perhaps ought) to be. One of the theatre's great gifts to humankind is imagining possibilities in the public square. Redemption, reinvention, transformation and second chances potentially lead a floundering juvenile delinquent toward living smarter with a literate mind. Such possibilities offer nobility to both student and teacher. Hector's eureka moments launch his early stage development and hold the chance for him to counteract his destructive habits. Ty's efforts as a teacher move the needle in Hector toward having a chance at becoming a better version of himself, even though the progress is in inches. Buoyed by a philosophy that everyone can make forward strides, Ty's work with Hector reaffirms his life calling to teach. In Ty's teacher's ethos, no one is beyond help; no one should be left behind. Hector's incremental growth is the metric of success that truly matters for teachers.

References

Bureau of Labor Statistics. U.S. Department of Labor. (2017). The economics daily. *Unemployment rate 2.5 percent for college grads, 7.7 percent for high school dropouts.* Retrieved from https://www.bls.gov/opub/ted/2017/unemployment-rate-2-point-5-percent-for-college-grads-7-point-7-percent-for-high-school-dropouts-january-2017.htm

Fontdevila, C., & Verger, A. (2019). The political turn of corporate influence in education: A synthesis of main policy reform strategies. In M. Parreira do Amaral, G. Steiner-Khamsi, & C. Thompson (Eds.), *Researching the global education industry: Commodification, the market and business involvement* (pp. 47–68). London: Palgrave Macmillan.

Georgetown Center on Education and the Workforce. (2018). Help wanted: Projecting jobs and education requirements through 2018. Retrieved from https://cew.georgetown.edu/cew- reports/help-wanted

Haynes, M. (2010, September 20). The federal role in confronting the crisis in adolescent literacy. Retrieved from https://all4ed.org/news/the-federal-role-in-confronting-the-crisis- in-adolescent-literacy/

Lake, R. (2016, May 12). Shocking facts: 23 statistics on illiteracy in America. Retrieved from https://www.creditdonkey.com/illiteracy-in-america.html

Mastrosimone, W. (1998). *Tamer of horses.* New York: (n.p.).

Mastrosimone, W. (2014). *Tamer of horses.* New York: (n.p.).

National Council of Adult Learning. (2015). Adult education facts that demand priority attention. Retrieved from http://www.ncalamerica.org/AdultEDFacts&Figures1215.pdf

The Room 241 Team. (2018, March 5). Crisis point: The state of literacy in America. Retrieved from https://education.cu-portland.edu/blog/education-news-roundup/illiteracy-in- america

Response to Chapter 4
The Teacher as Savior Fallacy

Shelley Nowacek

In *Tamer of Horses* (1993), Mastrosimone names the runaway young man fighting against institutional oppression – initially represented by society and later reflected in his teacher – after the Greek warrior, Hector. In Homer's *Iliad*, Hector is the hero, represented as an ideal warrior and the mainstay of Troy, a Trojan prince known as the Breaker of Horses. It is an ironic naming, as the reader's initial response to *Tamer of Horses* is to identify with Ty, the heroic, selfless teacher, rather than Hector, a difficult kid who hides a secret.

In his chapter, Ambush focuses on Ty. Ambush describes the heart of the play as an examination of the ethos of the teacher and the great lengths to which a teacher will go to try to reach a soul in trouble, even if that mission is distorted by corrupting influences – as seen later in *Tamer of Horses*. Ambush argues that teachers are virtuous and selfless and play a vital role in our social fabric. He also describes the principles and attitudes of this teacher's ethos as a rudder that steers a teacher's moral conduct, often at great personal cost, for the sake of a higher goal.

Though this could be argued as Ty's motivation, the greater argument tugging at the reader is Ty's symbolic representation of the endemic Great American Way: the idea that the current educational construct is the only salvation for lesser beings, misfits, women, even people of color. This theme rings cacophonously like thunder and delivers like prophesy through Ty's actions, aimed at Hector and Georgiane, as if they were children at the feet of Jesus in a Christian children's Bible pictorial, receiving the Word and redemption through divine forces. In presenting Ty as heroic and selfless, Ambush's chapter distorts the teacher's selfishness and danger to others and himself.

I would argue that it is a much more selfish and self-serving Ty that sets this play in motion, not a man driven by ethos as an educator. In Ty, the notion that education is the only salvation is revealed in his actions and his relationships with his wife and Hector. Although it appears that he has the student's best interests at heart, he forces his will onto an unsuspecting Hector, who is seeking refuge in the stables at the couple's home.

Hector, a natural poet but without the means to construct the written word, becomes hostage to Ty, as Ty requires an exchange for shelter in his world. Ty warns Hector that without reading, he is doomed to live a life of crime:

HECTOR: Who won?
TY: I'll lend you the book.
HECTOR: Ain't got time for no books, man. Who won?
TY: Can you read?
HECTOR: Don't be dissin' me, man!
TY: You want to learn?
HECTOR: Shit, no.
TY: I had a brother who couldn't read, and let me tell you where he ended up.

(Mastrosimone, 1993, pp. 265–266)

Ty then attempts to convince Hector that reading is the way to salvation through discussions that include Hector's song-selling strategy that someone else will do the work. Ty argues that, even though someone else can write down the lyrics to his songs, Hector still must learn to read so that he can take a driver's test to drive the motorcycle he plans to buy with the money he will make having someone else writing down his songs. Though it seems that Ty is initially interested in helping Hector, as the play continues, Ty uses blackmail to coerce Hector into learning:

TY: Well, laugh at this tough man: I got you by the balls. This is how it's going to be: You are up at six o'clock every morning.
HECTOR: All right, Ty.
TY: You do your chores.
HECTOR: All right, Ty.
TY: You take classes with me.
HECTOR: Classes?
TY: You learn how to read.
HECTOR: Shit!
TY: Or explain it to the police.

(Mastrosimone, 1993, p. 272)

The arguments prove too much for Hector and he snaps back at Ty verbally throughout the play. Hector fights to avoid Ty's educational deliverance through his actions, as well – by deflecting conversations regarding his learning, instigating conflict and, later, purposely breaking the law.

As many of us in education colloquially understand, coercion doesn't work in the classroom. Instead, students need a reason to want to learn: their future, a career aspiration, an interest. Keeping them on the straight and narrow path is not inspiring to students, yet this is Ty's approach with Hector. In their exchanges, Hector appears as a "sinner" in Ty's eyes and Ty plans to help Hector do his penance through learning.

Ty's own words reveal his real reason for wanting to teach: so that the world would reward him for "creating," much like God would create man and the world around him,

> I wanted to produce a one thinker, one dreamer, who could make the desert green, make the sea drinkable, or make a line of poetry that would outlast the centuries....at the end of the year, I used to wait in my classroom for one student, the one I got to, to come in my class after exams to say thank you. Thank you for giving me another world a bit better than the one I live in. But no student ever came to visit. Because I never got to no one. Not one. I didn't want to just teach students. I wanted to create them.
>
> (Mastrosimone, 1993, pp. 286–287)

Hector does "repent" initially and take the educational wafer offered by Ty. But as the play continues, Ty isn't able to re-"create" Hector, and when Ty fails to create Hector in his own image, he gives up on Hector and turns him in.

Is ethos at play here? I would argue the opposite: Ty as a teacher is not the embodiment of selflessness that he may at first seem but is, instead, using Hector to prove to himself that he is still valuable as a teacher. If viewed in this light, Ty is self-centered and selfish, using and manipulating Hector to prove his own self-worth. This self-centeredness (and myopic and self-interested view of Hector's arrival) seeps into his relationship with Georgiane, too.

In the following exchange between Hector, Georgiane and Ty, it is clear that there is tension – obvious tension in Hector's arrival and tension between Ty and Georgiane regarding Hector's arrival.

This tension reveals Ty's motivation and gives insight into Ty and Georgiane's marriage:

HECTOR: I don't care man. 'Least they ain't gonna be raggin' my ass out wit all kinds o' questions! [Exit Hector with his boombox blasting a rap song. Ty and Georgiane look at one another. Ty picks up Hector's bloody shirt.]

TY: Did you have to give him the third degree?

GEORGIANE: Ty, I only asked—

TY: I was here. I heard it. And I saw him run out the damn door.

GEORGIANE: Well, I think he's in big trouble.

TY: I think he needs a refuge, not an inquisition. (He throws Hector's bloody shirt on the floor, exits.)

GEORGIANE: Ty? (She picks up the shirt. Lights fade on Georgiane.)

(Mastrosimone, 1993, pp. 258–259)

Georgiane, approaching mid-life as a childless woman, appears to be, initially, an equal partner in her marriage, or even falsely in control of her husband at the beginning of the play; her actions with Hector, as seen above, appear to give her the upper hand in the exchanges between the men. However, she quickly becomes a pawn in taming the horse/reforming Hector. Though she seems to support Ty, she is skeptical and suspicious of Hector from the beginning, worried that "folks around here" (Mastrosimone, 1993, p. 268) will judge them for taking in a criminal and apprehensive that Hector will jeopardize the life they've worked so hard to build on the farm. She initially appears to want Hector to stay as a project for Ty, as if somehow this will be a starting place for the salvation of a troubled marriage:

TY: Why'd you ask him to stay?

GEORGIANE: I thought you wanted it. I thought you needed some company. I worry about you here alone all day long. I just don't know what to do anymore, Ty. We're losing each other.

(Mastrosimone, 1993, p. 268)

Georgiane and Ty both use Hector as a project: Georgiane initially uses him as company for Ty and Ty uses him as an investment for his own salvation. Once Georgiane hears of a burglary, however, she quickly distances herself and her emotional investment from Hector and his plight. Ty's investment runs more deeply; he is mired in the details and wants to save Hector, symbolically saving himself and simultaneously appearing as a savior.

To give of one's self is noble, but to give of one's self without boundaries – and at the risk of one's self – is foolish and perhaps ultimately tragic. Though teachers want the best for every student, they risk crossing ethical and sometimes moral boundaries by getting too close. This is where Ty is not operating in ethos but in foolishness and selfish self-centeredness. He is risking the possibility of returning to a teaching career, as well as the future of his family, to aid and abet a criminal. By the end of the play, he has clearly crossed boundaries and, should he be caught, he would lose his ability to teach after harboring a fugitive in his home.

However, Ty himself fails to see that he, too, is held hostage by falling prey to his own savior beliefs: He is desperate to remain a part of the educational institution that removes him from his teaching position. Before the play opens, Ty loses his job as a teacher when he resists changing a student's grades so that the student can enter an Ivy League institution. There is a certain irony that this play pre-dates the 2019 scandals of celebrities paying their children's way into prestigious colleges (Barrett & Zapotosky, 2019), including the Ivy League institutions that lead to Ty's downfall. With college costs at an all-time high, saddling students with high tuition costs and mountains of debt, is the institution of education the ultimate American success story now? Is Hector's learning to read his only salvation? Is education the only way to achieve the American Dream?

Ambush's argument has merit but it is limited in scope and accuracy for those of us who face the daily reality of public education. In *Tamer of Horses*, the limitations of what we see on the stage are replicated in what we believe about education. In Ambush's response, Ty is characterized as a teacher with an idealized vision of education and his place in that educational world. Ty fashions himself a savior, even when the reality is that Hector will not repent in the end. This archetypal savior-teacher on the stage keeps real teachers at arms' length, turning us against the non-relatable Ty and distancing us from his doctrine of education.

References

Barrett, D., & Zapotosky, M. (2019, March 12). FBI accuses wealthy parents, including celebrities, in college-entrance bribery scheme. *The Washington Post*. Retrieved from https://wapo.st/2J6Stzb?tid=ss_mail&utm_term=.5bde34b5e7c8

Mastrosimone, W. (1993). *Collected plays*. New York: Smith and Krauss.

5 Teaching the Coach, Coaching the Teacher

Richard St. Peter

Coaches in U.S. youth sports are volunteers, often parents, who may have little experience with coaching before they are thrust onto a field to improvise their way through practices and games. Coaches are familiar with the all-too-common refrain from parents: "How hard is it to coach? All you do is come up with a drill or two, and sit there in your chair and watch games. Anyone could do it" (O'Sullivan, 2014, p. 1). As Wikeley and Bullock (2006) argue, though,

> Coaches are educators in that their role is to work with one or more athletes in order to move the latter's performance to an improved level. Coaching is a process akin to teaching, tutoring or mentoring. It requires an understanding of the complex business of how people learn and develop as well as knowledge and skill in the discipline or field.
>
> (p. 14)

The legendary coach, John Wooden, also saw coaching as a form of teaching: "In the end, it's about the teaching...Not the games, not the tournaments, not the alumni stuff. But teaching the players during practice was what coaching was all about to me" ("Motivational quotes," n.d.).

Like teachers, coaches bring personal philosophies to their work with young people. When coaching philosophies collide on the same field – or dugout, as is the case in Richard Dresser's Little League baseball play *Rounding Third* – the resulting clashes call into question the fundamental values being taught to children in contemporary society.

Coach, Isn't that Cheating?

The genesis of Dresser's play – which premiered in 2002 at Northlight Theatre in Chicago and subsequently had a 2003

Off-Broadway run at the John Houseman Theatre – began when his son Sam came home from practice and told his father that the coach had a new strategy for the upcoming playoffs:

> When one of the slower kids on the team got on base, he'd receive a signal which meant that upon reaching the next base, he should slide and pretend to be injured. That way, the coaches could take him out of the game and replace him with a faster runner. When Sam said, "Coach, isn't that cheating?" the coach replied, "No, Sam, that's called strategy."
>
> (Dresser, 2002, p. 5)

Dresser was "horrified" by this pronouncement but he grew more understanding as he became more intimately involved with his son's team, first as an assistant coach and then eventually as the head coach. His philosophy at the beginning was clear: "Little League should be fun and the kids should be encouraged to progress at their own speed, free of the overwhelming pressure that awaits practically every aspect of their lives, just around the corner" (p. 5). Something happened on the way to the diamond, however: He realized he wanted to win. As he justified in his introduction to *Rounding Third* (2002), "Don't we have an obligation to teach our children now to succeed? Given that this is the arena where they will be playing out their lives, shouldn't we equip them with the tools it takes to win?" (p. 6). Dresser's philosophical shift comes to life in *Rounding Third*'s two characters: Don, a win-at-all-costs head coach, and Michael, his new assistant who wants the kids to have a great time playing the game.

Child's Play

In the years since Dresser wrote *Rounding Third*, playing youth sports for "fun" has reflected the growing inequality in the United States:

> Economic disparities and racial inequalities often mediate gender gaps in sport. High involvement with sports was more typical if kids came from wealthier, more affluent communities. Overall, kids from richer communities were more apt to play three or more sports.
>
> (Sabo & Veliz, 2016, p. 26)

In many sports, expensive travel teams have replaced organized youth leagues and the idea of a child moving from sport to sport throughout the calendar year has evolved (or devolved) to the idea of specialization at an early age. Children as young as eight often "choose" to concentrate on a single sport. As Thompson (2018) explains:

> As soon as some children enter second or third grade, their parents scramble to place them on youth travel teams, which will set them up for middle-school travel teams, which will set them up for high-school athletic excellence, which will make them more competitive for admissions and scholarships at select colleges. They then try out for or are selected to play on travel teams that form and stick together year-round.
>
> (p. 1)

The ever-escalating costs associated with these travel teams mean many children who come from families of more modest economic means are left behind. Thompson (2018), quoting Tom Farrey, the Executive Director of Aspen's Sports & Society program, lays it out: "Kids' sports has seen an explosion of travel-team culture, where rich parents are writing a $3,000 check to get their kids on super teams from two counties, or two states, away" (p. 1). By the time children reach middle school, youth sports are often divided between recreational leagues and travel teams. Children may also stop playing altogether, since the inadvertent segregation caused by travel teams has led to a significant decline in participation across all sports among children aged 6–12, with baseball participation down 20 percent from 2008 (Thompson, 2018).

Wouldn't You Rather Win than Lose?

Dresser's play begins with the two characters meeting for the first time. Don, a self-proclaimed successful Little League coach, and Michael, his new assistant coach, are discussing the upcoming season, with Don sharing one of the secrets to his coaching success:

DON: Mike, if there's one key to my personal success it would be this: I draft well.
MICHAEL: Nice going! (*Beat*). What exactly does that mean?

(Dresser, 2002, p. 11)

Michael's inexperience with coaching is clear: He has no idea what it means to draft players or how new players get on teams. Don reveals that his son Jimmy watches kids at school and clues his father in on whom to keep an eye on and whom to avoid. When Michael hears about Don's list of kids to avoid – "the ones who'd rather be in *Brigadoon*" (Dresser, 2002, p. 11) – Michael wants reassurance that all interested kids will get on a team. Don reassures him that Jimmy has reported favorably on Michael's son but, when he reads a scouting report of kids to avoid, one name catches Michael's attention: Frank Nassiter-Wise.

MICHAEL: I think we might have a little problem with Frank Nassiter-Wise.

DON: Oh, I'm sure we'd have many problems with Frank Nassiter-Wise if he ended up on the team. Which, may I say, is highly unlikely.

MICHAEL: He's my son.

(Dresser, 2002, p. 13)

Don is flummoxed when he learns that Michael is the boy's stepfather but Michael is more concerned that kids who want to play, but aren't as experienced, will be blackballed from the team – which is, in fact, not the case.

All youth who sign up for little league play are placed on teams; additionally, all players have to play a portion of each game and have at least one at-bat. Don is manipulating the system, however, by having his son – a good player – pay attention to other good players at school. Don can knowingly choose them for his team rather than picking potential bad players he doesn't know. Don's philosophy is simple: avoid the kids who can't play and "draft" the kids who are already talented. As he explains to Michael:

Nobody's blackballing anybody. My first obligation is to the kids. Every one of which will play, as long as they get here on time. But if I can field a better team, why shouldn't I? Wouldn't you rather win than lose, given the choice?

(Dresser, 2002, p. 14)

Michael is still not convinced that winning is as important as Don makes it out to be. Given their philosophical coaching differences, Don suggests Michael step down as his assistant coach but Michael declines to quit and Don reminds him to be on time for the first practice.

The Fun Is in the Playing

One of the conceits of Dresser's play is that the two coaches talk to the team through direct address to the audience, with individual audience members being addressed as players. In the next scene, Don addresses the "team" by laying out his expectations for the season:

> First, congratulations! You're the luckiest kids in town. You're on my team. I can promise you'll work hard, learn a lot, and have fun. How do we have fun playing baseball? One word. Winning. Winning is fun. Losing stinks. I hope this isn't new information.
>
> (Dresser, 2002, pp. 16–17)

He concludes with a brief explanation on the differences between physical errors, which are acceptable, and mental errors, which are emphatically not:

> Now, we all drop fly balls, miss grounders, make bad throws. That's baseball. Those are called physical errors, and I will never yell at you over physical errors. What is it called when we forget how many outs there are or throw to the wrong base? Anyone? Those are mental errors, and yes, my friends, you *will* hear from me about mental errors.
>
> (Dresser, 2002, p. 17)

At this point, Michael enters, late for practice, carrying two cups of coffee and fielding a call from work. After explaining to Don that his lack of baseball knowledge is thanks to growing up in Canada and only participating in curling, Michael addresses the team:

> It's about competition. These curling matches were the most important thing in my life when I was ten years old. But I honestly don't remember who won. I remember playing. So what I want to say to you, with the benefit of hindsight and, well, "wisdom" might be overstating it, is this: the fun is in the playing, not the winning and the losing. That's what I hope you will take away from this experience and what you will treasure when you get to be my age. And I guarantee you this, people, win or lose, you will have one heckuva lot of fun!
>
> (Dresser, 2002, p. 20)

Both coaches have now articulated competing philosophies to the team. Don is clearly focused on the now. Winning is what matters, therefore winning is fun; ergo, if the team wins, the team, by default, will have fun – but winning comes first. Michael is focused on the future. For him, the fun is in the experience of playing the game and what the will kids remember about their Little League experience years down the road. Their coaching philosophies represent the conflict of the play – and a common conflict found on the fields and courts of youth sports throughout the country.

As they prepare to leave practice, Michael realizes Don is staying behind to have his son Jimmy and another boy, Eric, work on their pitching. Dresser presents a different side to Don in this scene, one that serves to humanize Don for the audience and complicate him for Michael.

MICHAEL: Is this special attention or punishment?

DON: What does it look like to you, Mike? (*Yells to kids*) Jimmy, stop screwing around or you're dead meat!

MICHAEL: It's hard to say.

DON: Coaching your own kid is one of the hardest things a man can do. Too tough, people will talk, too nice, it's playing favorites. Plus, the kid thinks every nugget of advice is a vicious personal attack.

MICHAEL: Why is Eric here?

DON: He's been goofing off so I made him stay.

MICHAEL: Sounds like punishment.

DON: That's baseball.

MICHAEL: I should tell you, as assistant coach, I think these kids need to have fun. All this pressure and discipline is going to squelch their natural enthusiasm. We don't want that, do we?

DON: We certainly don't, Mike (*Yells*) No curve balls, Eric! Or you'll find yourself in the spring musical.

(Dresser, 2002, pp. 23–24)

This is one of the areas where coaching and teaching share common traits. For many coaches – and teachers – the job doesn't end when the practice is over. In his 2014 article, O'Sullivan asks rhetorically,

> Do you know how many hours a coach spends talking to players, not about only sport but about life? Do you realize how

many hours are spent dealing with a parents' divorce, a broken heart or problems with drugs or alcohol?

(p. 1)

As in many classrooms, the connection between teacher and student, coach and athlete, is not measured by the clock; the job doesn't end when the bell rings or the practice ends. The audience sees this concept reflected on stage when Michael confronts Don about going easier on Jimmy and Eric and, by extension, the rest of the team:

MICHAEL: Let's let them play on their own. Explore their imaginations, be the proud captains of their own little ships –
DON: Mike, did you happen to notice Eric's eye-twitch?
MICHAEL: No, I didn't.
DON: His parents just had a nasty split and neither one will the leave the house. Advice from their lawyers. Every day's trench warfare with Eric in the middle, looking for cover.
MICHAEL: Oh, boy. That's rough.
DON: His dad comes to all the games and yells about how disappointed he is. Gives everyone a nice boost. So when the eye-twitch is really bad, I make Eric stay after practice and we go out for pizza and he spends the night at our house. (*Yells*) Eric! Put your damn shoes back on or you're outta here! I'm not playing!
MICHAEL: That's a nice thing you're doing, Don.
DON: No, it's my job. I'd like to drag his idiot parents out of the house and kick their asses...

(Dresser, 2002, pp. 24–25)

O'Sullivan (2014) defines "coaches of positive significance" as those coaches who "realize that when you invest in people off the field, success on the field usually follows" (p. 1). He also argues that coaches of positive significance "no longer measure success in wins or losses, and in trophies and medals" (p. 1). However, knowing Don's previously established quest to win, should the audience assume he does this because he cares about Eric as a person or because he cares about Eric as a player? Perhaps more importantly, does his motivation matter if Eric benefits all the same?

This interaction complicates Don as a character as well as a coach. Where does his obligation to his players end? What is his responsibility to players after practice? In Act II, Don humorously asks Michael how much he thinks about the team when not at practice or a game. When a confused Michael doesn't answer right away, Don replies, "I would say with me it's fifty-five percent. Easy. Then I think about money maybe twenty-five percent of the time. The rest is all sex and revenge fantasies. You honestly don't know your percentages?" (Dresser, 2002, p. 55). Not surprisingly, Michael does not and he doesn't know how to respond to this admission.

Michael is also at a loss when he reveals that his wife died roughly a year earlier, leaving him to raise his stepson, Frankie. Rather than offering any sympathy, Don verbally lashes out at Michael, exclaiming,

> Jesus Christ! Look, Michael, in your candy-ass world you hand out Popsicles and tell all the kids they're great and nobody should ever feel bad. Now that's a helluva world but it isn't the real world. In the real world, everything's hard. Jobs are hard, money's hard, being alone is hard, being with someone else is impossible. Ever notice who the happy people are? Winners. Everyone else is thirty seconds away from blowing their goddamn brains out. You want to give these kids something? Make 'em winners. Give them a shot at a life that doesn't break their heart. That's the hardest thing you'll ever do.
>
> (Dresser, 2002, pp. 46–47)

To Don, being a 12-year-old Little League baseball champion prepares a child for the future; winning is the foundation by which young people successfully navigate their way to adulthood. This is why he coaches. Yet, Don walks away from the team in Act II.

Upset that Jimmy, his son and the star player, has been cast in *Brigadoon*, the school musical, and quit the team, Don unveils a strategy for the playoffs, the same one that prompted Richard Dresser to write the play: Slower players who reach base will fake an injury and be replaced by faster runners. Michael is incensed: "That isn't strategy. That's called cheating" (Dresser, 2002, p. 54). Despite Don's explanation that he is trying to make amends to the team for losing their star player, Michael pleads with him to "let them play, Don. Just let them play. It's ok" (p. 55). As their argument intensifies, Michael inadvertently reveals hearing Don's wife arrange an assignation with Don's best friend (and former assistant coach). Don explodes, quitting the team on the spot and leaving a bewildered Michael in charge. After fumbling over what to do with the team, Michael draws on his own philosophy of coaching: "Instead, let's just do what you guys want to do. Play ball. Count off, one, two, one, two, the ones play...the twos" (p. 61).

I Really Want to Win

Perhaps surprisingly, the team makes it to the championship game under Michael's leadership. When Don comes to the field on the day of the game, Michael convinces him to help out and shares a secret as the players warm up:

MICHAEL: I have a confession to make, Don.
DON: Oh? What's that?
MICHAEL: I really want to win.
DON: You're in the championship. You're already a winner.
MICHAEL: No, I know it's just another game and everything but I'm telling you, I really want to win.
DON: Hey, keep the kids relaxed and focused and who knows?
MICHAEL: No, you don't understand. I really really want to win

(Dresser, 2002, p. 65)

Michael has spent the entire season espousing the idea that wins and losses don't matter; as long as the kids have a good time and maybe learn a little something, all will be well. In coaching his team in the championship game, however, he finds winning matters a great deal more to him than expected. What hasn't changed, however, is the character Dresser establishes at the beginning of the play. Michael does want to win and is surprised by his newfound desire to win but, as Dresser demonstrates, he doesn't attempt to win at all costs: Michael remains true to his philosophy.

Late in the game, the opposing team loads the bases and there is a fly ball to right field, Frankie's position. The boy has struck out three times and had a ball get by him in the outfield. As the ball arcs toward its his stepson, the play pauses for Michael to say a prayer:

Dear God, please let him catch this ball. Just this once, let him know what it feels like to have the ball stay in his glove and not go bouncing past so he chases it in a mad terror with everyone screaming and when he finally finds it he has no idea what to do. We've done that. Many times. Let him catch this ball. Let him have this one memory for the rest of his life, that summer afternoon when the ball fell into his glove and stayed there. And let him jog back to the bench smiling in spite of himself, getting pats on the back from his teammates, still clutching the ball that didn't get away. He's never had that and he may never have the chance again. Check your stats, God, he's twelve years old, no team for my boy next year. So this is it.

(Dresser, 2002, p. 68)

Frankie has already struck out three times. He should conceivably be on the bench, replaced by a more competent player. Michael leaves him in and is prepared to face the consequences of his decision. Theatre doesn't always have to reflect life: Frankie makes the catch. As fate – and good playwriting – would have it, however, Michael does not get his championship: The tying run is thrown out at the plate to end the game. The season is over; it's time to pack up the equipment and go home for another year. As Dresser's final stage direction reads, *DON and MICHAEL sit on the bench in silence, not ready to let the season end. FADE TO BLACK* (Dresser, 2002, p. 72).

Until Next Season

What is the takeaway from this charming, bittersweet and funny two-hander? In 2007, I directed *Rounding Third* at Actors Guild of Lexington (KY) where I served as the Artistic Director. Before discovering theatre, I grew up playing youth sports, primarily baseball. I played for coaches similar to both Don and Michael in high school, college and semiprofessional leagues until I was 37. Directing the play was, for me, a tribute to all the Dons and Michaels for whom I played. To get at the heart of the competing coaching philosophies, the two actors I cast as Don and Michael – Adam Luckey and Scott Wichmann – learned both parts and alternated roles every night. A constant discussion in rehearsal centered on the idea of how switching roles allowed them to see the journey each character travels during the play. As the season progresses, Don and Michael slowly move toward each other. Michael wants the kids to have fun and realizes winning is fun. Don wants to win but discovers the humanity peeking out from underneath the baseball hats of his young players. These two characters – each described by Dresser only as "a man" – recognize that what is missing within themselves is in the other. They do not switch places, they do not even become friends but, in the end, they come to an understanding with each other and themselves.

What do we learn on a baseball field, basketball court, soccer pitch or football field and how does that translate to the rest of our lives? Kids are watching their coaches. What lessons are they learning? And what do those lessons say about our society? These questions get asked each time a new team takes the field regardless of the sport, the season or the score. Perhaps that is, in part, why we play the game.

References

Dresser, R. (2002). *Rounding third*. New York: Dramatic Publishing.

O'Sullivan, J. (2014, September 11). Are great coaches becoming an endangered species? *Changing the game project*. Retrieved from https://changingthegameproject.com/are-great-coaches-becoming-an-endangered-species/

Sabo, D., & Veliz, P. (2016). Surveying youth sports in America: What we know and what it means for public policy. In M. A. Mesner, & M. Musto (Eds.), *Child's play* (pp. 23–42). New Brunswick, NJ: Rutgers University Press.

Success Magazine. (n.d.). Motivational quotes: Coach John Wooden inspired the best of the best. Retrieved from https://www.thewoodeneffect.com/motivational-quotes/

Thompson, D. (2018, November 6). American meritocracy is killing youth sports. *The Atlantic*. Retrieved from https://www.theatlantic.com/ideas/archive/2018/11/income-inequality-explains-decline-youth-sports/574975/

Wikeley, F., & Bullock, K. (2006). Coaching as an educational relationship. In R. L. Jones (Ed.), *The sports coach as educator* (pp. 14–25). New York: Routledge.

Response to Chapter 5
Reading Coaches Critically

Luke Rodesiler

As a scholar who explores the critical study of sports and society in the context of literacy teaching and learning, I often find myself arguing that sports culture is a microcosm of our greater society and contending that sports-related texts can provide inroads into heady conversations about far-ranging sociopolitical issues and ways of being in the world. St. Peter's (2019) analysis of Richard Dresser's (2002) *Rounding Third* only strengthens my case. His breakdown illustrates that, though seemingly light fare, the fun, sports-based comedy featuring Little League coaches with competing visions about competition is actually rich with opportunities for exploring a host of weighty topics, among them, coaches' responsibility to the players in their care, the values kids learn by participating in sports and in society and the power dynamics between coaches and athletes.

Reading St. Peter's (2019) commentary on the two-man play calls to mind recent research Mark Lewis and I conducted as we investigated how coaches of organized youth sports are represented in works of young adult (YA) literature (see Rodesiler & Lewis, 2019). Extending Crowe's (2004) scholarship addressing the depiction of athletic coaches in YA literature, we analyzed a selection of 10 award-winning and/or recommended works of sports-related YA literature published over a 10-year span (2008–2017). Through our research, Mark and I identified the depiction of five distinct types of relationships between athletic coaches and adolescent-athletes: (a) coach-athlete; (b) mentor-protégé; (c) counselor-client; (d) victor-victim and (e) master-puppet.

The first three relationship types could be categorized as largely positive, yet each is nuanced. The coach-athlete relationship, which Mark and I illustrated with works such as *The Running Dream* (Van Draanen, 2011) and *Not if I See You First*

(Lindstrom, 2015), speaks to instances in which the coach is chiefly depicted fulfilling the duties that come with the job: helping athletes develop skills in their sport of choice and attending to athletes' health and wellbeing – little more, little less. The mentor-protégé relationship reflects instances in which a coach is shown guiding athletes outside the lines, as evinced in *Foul Trouble* (Feinstein, 2013) when Coach Wilcox advises star basketball player Terrell Jamerson as he experiences the ups and downs of the college recruiting process. On a more intimate level, the counselor-client relationship applies to depictions in which the coach supports athletes as they negotiate personal hardships, such as Coach Caledon aiding Hermione Winters following her rape at cheerleading camp in *Exit, Pursued by a Bear* (Johnston, 2016).

The two negative relationship types Mark and I identified through our research are also distinct. The victor-victim relationship describes instances in which the coach's pursuit of victory is detrimental to adolescent-athletes. The relationship between Coach Brigs and his players in *Leverage* (Cohen, 2011) is illustrative, as Brigs epitomizes the win-at-all-costs coach by taking seemingly every shortcut possible, from paying athletes and coaxing teachers to raise players' grades to supplying athletes with steroids and encouraging his team to injure the opposition. The master-puppet relationship also accounts for instances in which the coach manipulates adolescent-athletes; however, rather than doing so in the name of winning, the manipulative tactics in this relationship serve the coach's own personal benefit. For example, in *Foul Trouble* (Feinstein, 2013), Coach Stephenson attempts to steer top recruit Terrell Jamerson to the University of Atlanta not because the institution offers what Terrell desires for himself academically and athletically but because the coach has a new job waiting for him if he can deliver the basketball star.

St. Peter's (2019) analysis of Dresser's odd-couple play maps well onto the findings described above. Specifically, his take on Don, the experienced Little League coach whose embrace of a win-at-all-costs philosophy stands in stark contrast to the for-the-fun-it philosophy of his rookie assistant, suggests primarily a victor-victim relationship between the head coach and the players in his charge. Exploring further that particular representation of an athletic coach stands to extend the examination of coaches and teachers in dramatic works.

The Victor-Victim Relationship in *Rounding Third*

St. Peter's (2019) presentation and analysis of Don lays plain the head coach's priority: winning. Sure, Don pays lip service to prioritizing the players' wellbeing – "My first obligation is to the kids" – but the question he then poses to Michael, the team's new assistant coach, is telling: "Wouldn't you rather win than lose, given the choice?" Whether Don's pursuit of victory is for the benefit of the kids or for the coach himself is debatable; what is not in question is the fact that Don is willing to engage children in unethical practices for the sake of winning, as St. Peter describes,

> Upset that Jimmy, his son and the star player, has been cast in the school musical (*Brigadoon*) and quit the team, Don unveils a strategy for the playoffs, the same one that prompted Richard Dresser to write the play: Slower players who reach base will fake an injury and be replaced by faster runners.
>
> (p. 79)

St. Peter goes on to note Don's rationalization for the shortcut – "he is trying to make amends to the team for losing their star player" – yet no justification can excuse a coach corrupting the players in his care. In a victor-victim relationship between coaches and athletes, such corruption of sportsmanship and ethics is the price players pay so that, after the final out, coaches like Don can stand triumphantly with trophy in hand.

The Merit of Reading Coaches Critically

A reader's initial impulse might be to write off the negative representation of win-at-all-costs coaches like Don in Dresser's (2002) *Rounding Third* and to argue that such depictions do coaches a disservice by reinforcing negative stereotypes that we so often see in sports-related YA literature (e.g., Coach Brigs in *Leverage* [Cohen, 2011]), popular movies (e.g., John Kreese, sensei of the Cobra Kai dojo, in *The Karate Kid* [Weintraub & Avildsen, 1984]) and other media. Surely, such depictions don't do coaches any favors. However, as St. Peter's (2019) chapter demonstrates, a play like *Rounding Third* and its depiction of Don is vital because it provides an opportunity for reconsidering the fundamental values children are learning on the field of play and in our greater society. Do we compete to win? Do we stop at nothing to secure victory, on the field and off, or do we compete for the sheer joy of it? Should we just embrace the memories we make along the way – in sport and in life – rather than fret about winning and losing? Each is a question worthy of consideration, and that is especially true for prospective and practicing teachers and coaches, for their answers to such questions may have longstanding effects on the children they serve.

Educators must recognize that the merit of closely examining coaches is not limited to facilitating conversations about morals and ethics. Reading coaches critically also opens the door to studying issues of power and challenging figures who so often go unquestioned (Rodesiler & Lewis, 2019). Despite what the fan bases, trophy cases or press clippings of some might suggest, coaches are not infallible nor beyond reproach. For instance, in recent years, investigative reporting has revealed the verbal, physical and sexual abuses that rogue coaches have inflicted upon vulnerable athletes (e.g., see Abbott, 2018; Hauser, 2018), and it is often the power coaches wield that prevents athletes from speaking out sooner. Such realities underscore the value of inviting students to join us in critically reading coaches – on the stage, on the page and in daily life – and examining the power dynamics between coaches and athletes.

When we analyze power relations – including those of players and coaches, real or fictional – we investigate what is constructed as normal, attend to whose voices are silenced and whose are amplified and ultimately question who wins and who loses in those relationships (Janks, Dixon, Ferreira, Granville, & Newfield, 2014). By engaging in such critical analysis, we can position ourselves to "redesign" (Janks, 2014, p. 350) what it means to be a coach in the modern day and begin to normalize placing greater value on athletes' wellbeing than a coach's winning percentage. Fortunately, real-world athletes need not suffer for us to practice analyzing coaches critically; dramatic text and performance, young adult literature and other media provide ample opportunities for engaging in such important work.

References

Abbott, R. (2018). *The last days of Knight.* [Video]. Bristol, CT: ESPN+.

Crowe, C. (2004). *More than a game: Sports literature for young adults.* Lanham, MD: Scarecrow Press. https://watch.espnplus.com

Dresser, R. (2002). *Rounding third.* New York: Dramatic Publishing.

Hauser, C. (2018, May 15). Athletes who say volleyball coach abused them speak out. *The New York Times*. Retrieved from https://www.nytimes.com/2018/05/15/sports/volleyball -coach-sexual-abuse-illinois.html

Janks, H. (2014). Critical literacy's ongoing importance for education. *Journal of Adolescent & Adult Literacy, 57*(5), 349–356.

Janks, H., Dixon, K., Ferreira, A., Granville, S., & Newfield, D. (2014). *Doing critical literacy: Texts and activities for students and teachers*. New York: Routledge.

Rodesiler, L., & Lewis, M. A. (2019). "I thought coaches were supposed to set an example": Coaches' divergent roles in young adult literature. *The ALAN Review, 46*(2), 25–37.

St. Peter, R. (2019). Teaching the coach, coaching the teacher. In M. Shoffner, & R. St. Peter (Eds.), *Teacher representation in dramatic text and performance* (pp. 72–82). New York: Routledge.

Weintraub, J. (Producer), & Avildsen, J. G. (Director). (1984). *The karate kid* [Motion picture]. United States: Delphi II Productions.

Trade Books

Cohen, J. C. (2011). *Leverage*. New York: Dutton Books.

Feinstein, J. (2013). *Foul trouble*. New York: Alfred A. Knopf.

Johnston, E. K. (2016). *Exit, pursued by a bear*. New York: Dutton Books.

Lindstrom, E. (2015). *Not if I see you first*. New York: Poppy/Little, Brown.

Van Draanen, W. (2011). *The running dream*. New York: Alfred A. Knopf.

6   A Rocker in Teacher's Clothing
Outlandish Lessons in *School of Rock: The Musical*

Pauline Skowron Schmidt

People say that teaching is an art and that some teachers just have natural talent; this chapter aims to focus on a character who exhibits this natural talent, despite (technically) being a fraud. The character of Dewey Finn, in 2015's *School of Rock: The Musical*, pretends to be his roommate Ned Schneebly and accepts a substitute position at the prestigious Horace Green School. Thus starts the zany, musical adventure of "Mr. Schneebly" and an unsuspecting fifth grade class. When Dewey realizes that this particular group of students is musically inclined, he throws the traditional, rigorous curriculum out the window. He replaces all of it with "Rock Band" lessons, practice and analysis of rock and roll's legends, in an attempt to make his own dream of being a rock star come true.

This musical is based on the 2003 film of the same name, directed by Richard Linklater and starring the frenetic Jack Black. There are many similarities between the two iterations, but the soundtracks are notably different. The film is filled with familiar rock songs while the stage production embeds original songs for the characters to perform, thus revealing more of the backstory to certain characters, especially Principal Mullins. The film focuses on the relationship between teacher and students while relegating parents to minor roles; in the stage production, the parents appear as a unified force and secondary character. The stage musical also adds depth to the parent-student relationships through dialogue and musical numbers.

This chapter critically analyzes the character of Dewey Finn as he appears in the Broadway musical, examining his role as a substitute teacher despite his lack of formal teacher education. Using song lyrics from the show as subheadings, my analysis focuses on the following areas: background information and setting the proverbial stage, the curriculum and the school itself, the teacher's role and, finally, the impact on the students.

"He's Not Even a Teacher!"

When the curtains open on the audience's first view of the protagonist, they reveal an actual rock band, front and center stage; strobe lights float across the audience; electric guitars blast out a song called "I'm Too Hot for You." Misguided, but passionate, Dewey Finn thinks he is one of the greatest musicians ever; as the stage directions capture, "Dewey begins to play a wild guitar solo. His band mates watch in horror" (Webber, Slater, & Fellowes, 2015, p. 3). The audience quickly learns that his band is frustrated with him commandeering the spotlight while his roommate Ned is frustrated with him taking advantage of their living arrangement. Dewey is a dreamer at best, a slacker at worst. Either way, he is not teacher material.

Ned, as a responsible adult, is easily and appropriately identified as a substitute teacher who hopes to one day obtain a classroom of his own. While Ned goes off to work, Dewey goes off to band practice, only to be kicked out of the band he created. He then saunters into his part-time job at a record store, only to be fired there as well. Dewey returns home after singing "When I Climb to the Top of Mount Rock," vowing to pursue his dream of making music, when the phone rings. Principal Rosalie Mullins of the Horace Green Prep School is looking for Ned: she is in urgent need of a substitute teacher. When she mentions the pay is 950 dollars a week, Dewey quickly decides to be Ned-Schneebly-The-Substitute-Teacher. The audience doesn't see a scene where Dewey provides any identification; the officials at Horace Green Prep School assume the person who shows up is the substitute teacher Ned Schneebly and they put him into a classroom immediately.

I want to articulate a clear awareness that Dewey Finn enters the classroom illegally and without proper teacher training or certification; this is a fictional tale, after all. While there are several events in this story that would rarely happen in the real world, this chapter argues that despite legal ramifications, Dewey Finn does actually teach us a few important things about teachers and students.

"What Kind of Sick School Is This?"

As the musical continues, the audience can easily identify Horace Green Prep School as a private school catering to an elite social class. In one frenzied scene, parents drop off their children at the beginning of the school day. Many ask very specific questions of the principal about their child, with the expectation that the principal is able to answer these questions because she knows what is going on with every student.

What Dewey sees when he arrives, however, is the rigidity, routine and standardization of the school. He is appalled that students' achievements and wrongdoings are literally on display for all to see. Without having the foundational knowledge, he is seeing Freire's banking model at work. All of the students are passively receiving the same knowledge in the same ways, without ever being asked to think critically or question the content (Freire, 1993). In another scene, one of the students, Summer Hathaway, questions Dewey's ability to teach them while simultaneously mentioning that the tuition is $50,000 per year (Webber et al., 2015, p. 20). These parents, and subsequently, these children tie the tuition amount to a quantitative level of excellence they expect from that high price.

This pricey education echoes the stance of current Secretary of Education Betsy DeVos who has implied that, when she invests in something, she expects a return on that investment. According to a 2017 article in *The Washington Post*,

> In 1997, [DeVos] wrote in Roll Call, a publication covering Congress: "My family is the biggest contributor of soft money to the Republican National Committee. I have decided to stop taking offense," she wrote, "at the suggestion that we are buying influence. Now I simply concede the point. They are right. We do expect something in return. We expect to foster a conservative governing philosophy consisting of limited government and respect for traditional American virtues. We expect a return on our investment."
>
> (Strauss)

This type of entitlement can be problematic, particularly when the investors are not properly trained in any educational policy; in the musical production, none of the parents are identified as educators themselves. Yet the dialogue that takes place implies that they are in charge, they think they know what is pedagogically sound and they are entitled to the education they have paid for. Ironically, Betsy DeVos advocates for school choice because "too many kids are trapped in a school that's not meeting their needs" (American Federation for Children), yet none of the children at Horace Green seem to be trapped at this school. The trappings seem to occur within the strict, rigorous curriculum.

Beyond the financial context is the culture of perceived success; the song "Horace Green Alma Mater," sung by the children, uses the following terms: succeed, perfection, lock-step, excellence, pressure, funding and routine (Webber et al., 2015, p. 12). The lyrics of the song imply conformity in terms of how success is measured. Standardization is preferred, with students blending in rather than standing out. This curriculum does not seem responsive or even flexible enough to meet individual students' needs. When the song is reprised later in the show, it is sung by the faculty members. The lyrics echo the same focus, especially when the teachers sing, "our purpose is to glean good test results/from pre-adults/making sure each child is drilled/ and ranked and filed by score" (Webber et al., 2015, p. 49). It's clear that the teachers aren't thinking critically about what they are teaching, how they are teaching it or to whom they are teaching. Referring to children using these cold, calculated and quantitative ways should give the audience pause. Educators know that there are things that can't be measured; empathy, kindness, creativity, for example, are all things we value for students. These are all qualities that seem ignored, or at least not cultivated, in the environment of Horace Green, however.

In contrast to the highly trained expert teachers at Horace Green, we see Dewey question these exact notions in his song, "Stick it to the Man." He helps his students identify the forces in their lives that frustrate them – in this case, the pressure embedded at the school and at home. In a call and response song, Dewey sings "Stand up to the system...Rise up and resist 'em" with the students responding "Stick it to the Man" after each short line (Webber et al., 2015, p. 57). While some might say he's cultivating his own system of anarchy, he's also asking students to think critically about who they are and what they want for themselves.

Educational expert Sir Ken Robinson likes to pose the question, "What is education for?" (2015) and then explore the potential possibilities when it comes to answering his own question. He worries that our quest for meeting standards has gone too far: "instead of being a means of educational improvement, standardized testing has become an obsession in itself" (Robinson, 2015, p. 160). As the faculty of Horace Green sing, "We groom achievers/keep them focused/Minimize their quirks" (Webber et al., 2015, p. 50), we hear exactly what these teachers think education is for. There is also an element of questioning the status quo; why question it when it seems to be working for this elite upper class. Had this story taken place in a middle or working class school, or a public school, perhaps the storyline would take a different turn.

"You're Not Hardcore, Unless You Live Hardcore"

People come to the profession of education for a variety of reasons, some altruistic, some idealistic, some pragmatic. Dewey answers the substitute phone call with a very rudimentary cause: money. So, while most educators believe that "the reward of teaching is knowing that your life can still make a difference" (Ayers, 2010, p. 37), Dewey merely sees a paycheck. And yet Dewey Finn unknowingly teaches three key lessons to us as educators: passion for the specific content you are teaching; having in depth content knowledge and keen student knowledge and appreciation.

First, he brings an immense amount of passion for music to the classroom. As an audience member, watching the actor who played Dewey Finn in the musical production was an absolutely exhausting experience. His frenetic energy was apparent as he bounced around every part of the stage, singing, playing guitar and dancing around his young students. Passion is essential for all teachers; we must be passionate about our content area(s) or we will not be able to engage our students in making meaning. If teachers are 'leaders' and students are 'players', "the leader [must] be authentic in the process...[and] should model positive involvement in the experience. Children are perceptive and they will recognize false enthusiasm" (Rubin & Merrion, 2011, pp. 3–4). The passion exhibited by Finn seems innate in his personality; that is to say, no one trained him to be passionate about music.

The sheer number of musicians he names in the stage production is hard to calculate. Without a doubt, he knows his subject area: he is certainly a content specialist! Educators must know their content, broadly and specifically. English Language Arts teachers, for example, must know new work being done by specialists in the field as well as modern texts being written for adolescents. Before entering the classroom, they must study literature, writing and pedagogy so they can be considered content specialists.

Without recognizing this as an educational strategy, Dewey exhibits his own content knowledge when he distributes 'mentor texts' for his students to listen to and make connections to their own music. Ruth Culham (2014) writes about this notion of mentor texts in the context of a writing classroom: students read the professional text, first as readers, then as writers, looking at the stylistic elements and trying to mimic that in their own writing. Dewey applies this approach to music. Zach, the guitar player, is given an Eric Clapton CD; Freddy, the drummer, is given a RUSH CD; Billy, the band's stylist, is given David Bowie's iconic Ziggy Stardust album. These CDs provide the students with an epitome of their assigned skill or technique. The expectation is that the students will listen to appreciate the artist but then also be able to borrow the style and apply it to their own work. In sharp contrast to Friere's (1993) banking model, Finn embodies and implements Vygotsky's (1978) theory of play, allowing students to explore these musical icons and apply what they've heard in their own musical performances.

Beyond knowing our content, teachers must know our students' strengths and weaknesses. In the song "You're in the Band," Dewey quickly assesses the students' strengths and assigns tasks that highlight those strengths. He takes the passion he has for music and assembles his rock band, singing, "take a look at this music and let your mind expand" (Webber et al., 2015, p. 33). Within minutes, he assembles band members, singers, roadies, a tech crew, security and stylist. Summer, for example, becomes the band manager since she has already displayed strong leadership qualities. Dewey not only adapts to the students, but he also adapts the curriculum in a way that allows for the students to grow as individuals and as a community of learners. In a goodwill gesture, he invites the students to "talk about your influences" (p. 46) so they can start to consider what kind of rock band they collectively are. This experience echoes what Sir Ken Robinson (2015) meant when he suggested teachers leave room in education for students to pursue their own interests and strengths. This notion effectively pushes back on the standardization movement and focuses on learners as individuals.

Yet while Dewey tries to learn about his students' musical tastes, he mocks their choices. He is baffled by some of their preferences and revisits the rock legends to help illustrate his point. Perhaps, with formal teacher education training, he would know that mocking students is not an option in the classroom; teachers guide students to make more sophisticated or appropriate choices through modeling and exposure, never through ridicule. As teachers, knowing the curriculum and knowing the students are equally important but it's also paramount to establish a safe space for all students to feel comfortable sharing their interests.

"I Pledge Allegiance to the Band"

When Dewey first arrives in the classroom, he notices a giant poster with all the students' names and corresponding gold stars that track achievements. He is very upset with this visual representation of achievements and shortcomings – a visual representation of Freire's (1993) banking model – and rips it up, telling students that this is a tool of 'The Man'. Again, unknowingly, Dewey has adopted the growth mindset approach of Carol Dweck (Yeager & Dweck, 2012). She compares and contrasts 'fixed' and 'growth' mindset, with growth as the preferred approach. Dewey's approach falls short, however, when he says there will be "no grades and no gold stars and absolutely no achievements" (Webber et al., 2015, p. 21). While teachers want students to achieve, even more importantly, "a central task for parents and educators is to prepare students to respond resiliently when challenges arise" (Yeager & Dweck, 2012, p. 312).

Some lessons are qualitative in nature; it could be the nature of this class as it evolves from a typical fifth grade class to the focus on Rock Band. As Dewey is creating the plea to the students, he passionately exclaims, "Music speaks to you! That's what matters!" (Webber et al., 2015, p. 30). Students learn to grapple with these abstract concepts of what really matters as learners. They still experience growing pains as they move from their over-scheduled day to what they perceive as "goofing off" (p. 53). They are having fun during the school day, in part because they are focused on an enjoyable task. As Taljaad (2016) explains, they are "in the flow" where time passes because one is so intensely focused and immersed in the activity. Dewey explains that they are actually doing work – creating musical fusion – but they aren't used to this kind of learning and teaching. They are completely out of their comfort zone as learners.

However, Dewey encourages the students to be comfortable in their own skin and to really own who they are as individuals. Even though these students are self-proclaimed over-achievers, he helps them see that they are simply going through the motions associated with school. By Act Two, they learn that excelling does not necessarily equate with being excellent, illustrating Dweck's growth mindset in a very practical way. Dewey encourages these pre-teens to question authority and truly think for themselves. While the "Horace Green Alma Mater" touts concepts like excellence, discipline and routine, it is Dewey's teaching that truly embodies what it means to be excellent in education. His teaching transcends the classroom as his students find their voice(s) in the song "If Only You Would Listen," which illustrates that even kids have something to say, if only adults would listen.

"If Only You Would Listen"

The parents play an important role in the Broadway production. The audience sees them during drop off and pick up scenes, as well as in vignette scenes with kids and their respective parents. We also see the parents through Dewey Finn's eyes – he sees extremely high expectations and sometimes misplaced expectations, with parents projecting their own missed opportunities onto their children. For some of these parents, their focus on tradition and high expectations creates heartbreaking scenes. Freddy's dad yells about how much money he spends at Horace Green and how frustrated he is that Freddy only wants to focus on his music. The audience sees the father's comparison of growing up in a working-class environment to Freddy's living a life of privilege and avoidance of real work. This scene fades to Billy and his dad, who sees Billy as a football player. While Billy claims to be reading *Sports Illustrated*, the audience sees that the magazine is actually *VOGUE*. Billy clearly has a flair for designing the band's costumes, not playing or even watching football.

The children plead with their parents in the song "If Only You Would Listen" to really see them for who they are. The parents are too caught up in their own worlds to pay attention to their children but the kids insist, "I've got so much to share/If only you would listen/You could prove that you care/If only you would listen" (Webber et al., 2015, p. 45). This is one of the few ballads in the show and it speaks to the universal experiences between children and parents: not just tolerance but acceptance of all kids, especially our own. No one wins when parents slap unrealistic expectations or their own failed dreams onto their children. Children have to find themselves, no matter what that looks like.

In one of the final scenes, after Dewey is exposed as a fraud, the children commandeer a school bus and go to his apartment to pick him up so they can compete in the Battle of the Bands. To demonstrate that they are finally thinking critically, they perform the reprise of the song "If Only You Would Listen." Tomika sings, "You raised my voice up/ Taught me not to fear/ I've learned who I am/ Because you're here," followed by Lawrence singing, "I needed a chance/ Only you would listen" and then Summer, with, "I needed respect/ And only you would listen" (Webber et al.,

2015, pp. 103–104). The students didn't experience this kind of interaction before Dewey arrived on the scene at Horace Green. They didn't feel that the adults in their lives were seeing them or hearing what they had to say.

Dewey illustrates the essential component of student-teacher relationships, which every teacher approaches in their own way. Perhaps they bond over popular culture, books, music or sports but teachers must find a way to see students and actually appreciate their interests. While some might argue that this is a part of teaching that can't be taught, teachers will develop their own genuine style as they head into their own classrooms.

"I Believe the Children Are Our Future"

After day one, Dewey returns home to the apartment he shares with Ned and tells him that teaching is "life-sucking" (Webber et al., 2015, p. 23), yet he returns the next day. Just as real teachers do, Dewey connects with his students, referring to them as 'my kids' (p. 27). Particularly after the reprise of the "If Only You Would Listen," the audience can see how the teacher and students have bonded. As Robinson (2015) points out, Finn has extended opportunities for inspiration, confidence and creativity to the students (p. 127). By the end of the show, they know who they are and what they want to do: compete in the Battle of the Bands along with other (real) rock bands.

While unconventional at best, the lessons embedded in *School of Rock: The Musical* still apply to the teaching profession. Teachers must know their content, be passionate about it and actually like the kids in their classroom. Teachers must also understand the context and culture of the school and allow all students' opportunities to use their voices. According to Robinson (2018), "innovative schools everywhere are breaking the mold of convention to meet the best interests of their students, families, and communities" (p. 206). Dewey Finn as Mr. Schneebly helps us see that breaking the mold often means returning to what teaching really means: fostering relationships and seeing how that eclipses content on any given day.

References

American Federation for Children. (2018). School choice in America. *American Federation for Children*. Retrieved from https://www.federationforchildren.org/school-choice-america/

Ayers, W. (2010). *To teach: The journey of a teacher.* New York: Teachers College Press.

Culham, R. (2014). *The writing thief: Using mentor texts to teach the craft of writing.* Portsmouth, NH: Stenhouse Publishers.

Freire, P. (1993). *Pedagogy of the oppressed.* New York: Continuum Books.

Linklater, R. (Director). (2003). *School of rock* [Motion Picture]. Hollywood, CA: Paramount Pictures.

Robinson, K. (2015). *Creative schools: The grassroots revolution that's transforming education.* New York: Penguin Books.

Robinson, K. (2018). What happens to student behavior when schools prioritize art. *KQED News.* Retrieved from https://www.kqed.org/mindshift/50874/what-happens-to-student-behavior-when-schools-prioritize-art

Rubin, J. E., & Merrion, M. (2011). *Creative drama and music methods: Activities for the classroom* (3rd ed.). Lanham, MD: Rowman & Littlefield Publishers, Inc.

Strauss, V. (2017). She's a billionaire who said schools need guns to fight bears. Here's what you may not know about Betsy DeVos. *The Washington Post.* Retrieved from https://www.washingtonpost.com/news/answer-sheet/wp/2017/02/07/shes-a-billionaire-who-said-schools-need-guns-to-fight-bears-heres-what-you-may-not-know-about-betsy-devos/?utm_term=.a33217338171

Taljaad, T. (2016). The science of being in the flow. *Uplift Connect.* Retrieved from https://upliftconnect.com/being-in-the-flow/

Vygotsky, L. (1978). *Mind in society: The development of higher psychological processes.* Cambridge, MA: Harvard University Press.

Webber, A. L. (Music), Slater, G. (Lyrics), & Fellowes, J. (Script). (2015). *The next generation: School of rock the musical.* New York: The Musical Company.

Yeager, D. S., & Dweck, C. S. (2012). Mindsets that promote resilience: When students believe that personal characteristics can be developed. *Educational Psychologist, 47*(4), 302–314.

Response to Chapter 6
The Danger of Deweys: What Real Teachers Face

Lisa Scherff

Although commenting on a (very) fictional situation, Schmidt's chapter has relevance for K-12 education and teacher education. While it seems hardly feasible that a slacker/pseudo-musician such as Dewey can walk into a school with no identification and become a substitute teacher, he is able to accomplish quite a bit with the students. As Schmidt details, fictional Dewey is successful for real reasons: his passion for the subject matter, his ability to connect with students and his creation of an engaging curriculum.

However, media portrayals of teachers like Dewey are just that: fictionalized accounts that fail to present an accurate representation of not only the daily demands of the job but also the realities that classroom teachers face – and there is a danger in mythical teachers becoming the illusory standard by which many actual teachers are viewed and judged. While I admire the innate teacher qualities Dewey possesses, I want to complicate and counter this representation with the issues that real teachers face.

Like Dewey in the musical, good teachers possess not only content knowledge and a passion for their subject and their students but also pedagogical content knowledge (PCK). PCK is knowing how to teach the specific academic discipline with specific subject-matter ideas and strategies (Bransford, Brown, & Cocking, 2000; Neumann, Kind, & Harms, 2018; Shulman, 1986). PCK does not happen by accident; it develops through extensive preparation and practice.

Glimpses into and snapshots of "good" teaching on stage, while inspirational, do not accurately capture or advance the depth and breadth of preparation, skill and ability it takes to be a good teacher – and this sends a dangerous and misleading idea of teaching: that anyone can do it and do it well. If we are to believe Dewey, who needs training when anyone off the street can succeed?

However, teacher preparation matters. In a seminal analysis of teacher preparation by Wilson, Floden and Ferrini-Mundy (2001), the authors came to several conclusions:

- There is a positive association between subject matter preparation – both content and teaching methods – and teacher performance.
- Pedagogical preparation positively influences teaching and student learning.
- While the types of clinical experiences can vary widely, certified teachers consider them extremely effective.

In short, the more preparation teachers have, the more effective they will be. Effective teacher preparation programs include both clinical and didactic curricula, ensuring that candidates have the chance to learn the theoretical tools of teaching, such as knowledge of curriculum and materials, planning and organizing instruction, and developing assessment strategies, as well as the "opportunities to practice with these tools systematically" (Darling-Hammond, 2010, p. 40). Graduates of teacher education programs consider themselves better prepared and, consequently, add more to student learning (Darling-Hammond & Bransford, 2005).

Comparatively, research shows that teachers who enter the profession through short-term alternative routes are not as well prepared, and they do not stay in the profession as long and/or long enough to make it through the novice period (Darling-Hammond, Holtzman, Gatlin, & Heilig, 2005). Recent data also suggest that teachers with less preparation leave the profession at rates two to three times as high as those who have been through a comprehensive preparation program (Sutcher, Darling-Hammond, & Carver-Thomas, 2016).

As Schmidt shows, Dewey is able to translate and transfer his knowledge and love of music to the students, who exemplify this through their passion and playing, and they blossom because of it. So, while charismatic, energetic teachers like Dewey may succeed in the short term, their long-term viability is questionable. And that is an important point for students in the classrooms of such teachers, since research shows that it is not students attending well-resourced private schools that are taught by underprepared teachers but those who attend high-poverty schools and/or schools with a high number of students of color (Darling-Hammond, Sutcher, & Carver-Thomas, 2017).

Would Dewey be as successful at an under-resourced school – with not enough instruments to go around and no music room – or a school with a majority of students who read several grades below where they should or where many students do not speak English? As many have reported (i.e., Redding & Smith, 2016; Sutcher, Darling-Hammond, & Carver-Thomas, 2019; Sutcher et al., 2016), poor students, students of color and low-performing students are "disproportionately taught by less qualified teachers" and in "apartheid schools serving more than 90% students of color, a majority of teachers are inexperienced and uncertified" (Darling-Hammond, 2010, p. 38). Reason would have it, then, that such students are not offered the varied and rich curriculum (and instruction) that they deserve.

Schmidt (2019) rightly problematizes the issue of a narrow curriculum and notes the "rigidity, routine and standardization of the school" (p. 90) where Dewey is substitute teaching. However, standardization – in a school with vast resources like Horace Green – means something very different to many schools across this country. In countless schools, standardization is often scripted curricula, narrow pacing guides to keep teachers in check, and routinized dull practice for high-stakes tests.

As a classroom teacher, I have experienced this firsthand. As I reported recently (2018), my school district began a 1:1 Chromebook initiative during the 2016–2017 school year. The idea, as my fellow initial technology leaders and I were told, was to use the computers for more authentic teaching and learning: problem/project-based activities, differentiated instruction, extension activities. However, that vision changed when we began using them (i.e., were told) to give online assessments in reading and math every quarter. Then, we were told to use mandated online teaching modules, 15 minutes per week in every class, based on these "formative" assessments. Students who were behind their peers – often impoverished students, non-native speakers and students of color – had to complete more modules. Students in the advanced, honors and special programs classes, such as International Baccalaureate and Cambridge, were exempted from these practices. One only needed to look at the faces in these upper level classes to see disparities between and among demographic groups: "each year, more than half a million low-income students and students of color are 'missing' from AP and IB participation – students who would benefit from these advanced opportunities if they participated at the same rate as other students" (Theokas & Saaris, 2013, p. 3).

As a teacher at a private school, Dewey does not have to face mandated high-stakes assessments, which often negatively impact teaching and learning. He is free to teach what he likes and what will engage the students (although he does face criticism by students and parents). Most educators do not have that luxury. In states with graduation exams, for example, schools and teachers are evaluated and rewarded (or punished) based on student performance. Schools with high percentages of poor students and/or students of color often have lower test scores than schools that are wealthier or attended by white students (Boschma & Brownstein, 2016). Thus, many schools implement unsound teaching practices to raise their scores (e.g., McNeil, 2000; Nichols & Berliner, 2007; Ravitch, 2010).

Recently, I was interviewed by *Phi Delta Kappan* (Heller, 2019) about the state of English and challenges with/in instruction, issues outlined above that do not always wind up in film and on stage: narrow test-preparation curriculum, high-stakes testing, the amount of preparation it takes to learn to be an effective teacher. Although specifically about one subject area, other content areas have also faced similar challenges:

> A lot has changed over 15 years, though, given all the testing and accountability. I've asked a lot of my colleagues about this, and their responses have been sobering...a friend who teaches history said he doesn't see students doing any deep reading anymore...students tell him they're assigned just to read short excerpts and pull out evidence to answer test questions... another colleague who has taught English for 15 years [said] students are doing little to no extended writing, no process writing, no research papers. She's convinced that only the Advanced Placement students are actually being prepared to succeed in college. Even in the honors classes, she's made to teach canned assignments, which nobody enjoys.
>
> (p. 48)

So, while it is entertaining and perhaps a bit inspiring to watch teachers like Dewey on stage, the public must remember that real educators need time and preparation to become skilled, must follow established (external) guidelines and norms and face criticism and threats from outsiders who do not understand the day-to-day realities of the classroom.

102 *Lisa Scherff*

References

Boschma, J., & Brownstein, R. (2016). The concentration of poverty in American schools. Retrieved from https://www.theatlantic.com/education/archive/2016/02/concentration-poverty-american-schools/471414/

Bransford, J. D., Brown, A. L., & Cocking, R. R. (2000). *How people learn: Brain, mind, experience, and school.* Washington, DC: National Academy Press.

Darling-Hammond, L. (2010). Teacher education and the American future. *Journal of Teacher Education, 61*(1–2), 35–47.

Darling-Hammond, L., & Bransford, J. (Eds.). (2005). *Preparing teachers for a changing world: What teachers should learn and be able to do.* San Francisco, CA: Jossey-Bass.

Darling-Hammond, L., Holtzman, D. J., Gatlin, S. J., & Heilig, J. V. (2005). *Does teacher preparation matter? Evidence about teacher certification, Teach for America, and teacher effectiveness.* Retrieved from https://www.nctq.org/nctq/research/1114011196655.pdf

Darling-Hammond, L., Sutcher, L., & Carver-Thomas, D. (2017, November). Why addressing teacher turnover matters. Retrieved from https://learningpolicyinstitute.org/blog/why-addressing-teacher-turnover-matters

Heller, R. (2019). What is English? Who decides? An interview with Lisa Scherff. *Phi Delta Kappan, 100*(6), 45–49. Retrieved from https://www.kappanonline.org/english-curriculum-who-decides-interview-scherff-heller/

McNeil, L. M. (2000). *Contradictions of school reform: Educational costs of standardized testing.* New York: Routledge.

Neumann, K., Kind, V., & Harms, U. (2018). Probing the amalgam: The relationship between science teachers' content, pedagogical and pedagogical content knowledge. *International Journal of Science Education.* doi:10.1080/09500693.2018.1497217

Nichols, S. L., & Berliner, D. C. (2007). *Collateral damage: How high-stakes testing corrupts America's schools.* Cambridge, MA: Harvard Education Press.

Ravitch, D. (2010). *The death and life of the great American school system: How testing and choice are undermining education.* New York: Basic Books.

Redding, C., & Smith, T. M. (2016). Easy in, easy out: Are alternatively certified teachers turning over at increased rates? *American Educational Research Journal, 53*(4), 1086–1125.

Shulman, L. (1986). Those who understand: Knowledge growth in teaching. *Educational Researcher, 15*(2), 4–14.

Sutcher, L., Darling-Hammond, L., & Carver-Thomas, D. (2016). *A coming crisis in teaching? Teacher supply, demand, and shortages in the U.S.* Palo Alto, CA: Learning Policy Institute. Retrieved from http://

learningpolicyinstitute.org/sites/default/files/product-files/A_Coming_
Crisis_in_Teaching_REPORT.pdf

Sutcher, L., Darling-Hammond, L., & Carver-Thomas, D. (2019). Understanding teacher shortages: An analysis of teacher supply and demand in the United States. *Education Policy Analysis Archives*, 27(35). doi:10.14507/epaa.27.3696

Theokas, C., & Saaris, R. (2013). *Finding America's missing AP and IB students*. Washington, DC: The Education Trust. Retrieved from https://edtrust.org/wp-content/uploads/2013/10/Missing_Students.pdf

Wilson, S., Floden, R., & Ferrini-Mundy, J. (2001). *Teacher preparation research: Current knowledge, gaps, and recommendations*. Center for the Study of Teaching and Policy—A University of Washington, Stanford University, University of Michigan, and University of Pennsylvania consortium. Retrieved from https://www.education.uw.edu/ctp/sites/default/files/ctpmail/PDFs/TPExecSummary-03-2001.pdf

7 A Holey Trinity

Crises of Communion in John Patrick Shanley's *Doubt*

Jeff Spanke

Baptism

"What do you do when you're not sure," asks Father Flynn in the opening line of John Patrick Shanley's 2004 drama, *Doubt: A Parable*. "That's the topic of my sermon today." And indeed, the notion of navigating uncertainty anchors not only the remainder of the middle-aged Flynn's sermon but also the nuanced and unnerving events that follow in its wake.

Set in the immediate aftermath of the Kennedy assassination, and in the midst of an unprecedented paradigm shift in the Catholic church (O'Malley, 2010), *Doubt* centers around one nun's crusade to expose what she believes to be the systemic and habitual misconduct of her male superior at their Bronx Catholic school. Through extensive, questionably unethical reconnaissance and persistent coercion of another less-experienced and far-more reluctant nun (also a teacher), Sister Aloysius wages a compelling, though baseless, campaign against the head priest, grounded in certainty, while having no proof – or evidence – to offer.

Aside from the obvious parallels between Shanley's fictional 1964 St. Nicolas scandal and the all-too-real modern accounts at the time of child abuse at the hands of clergy (Rezendes, 2002), *Doubt's* 2004 premiere also coincided with one of the most profound shifts in American educational policy over the last half-century. Just as the assassination of President Kennedy ushered in a series of enemies (real or imagined, foreign or domestic) to Americans' collective sense of identity, unity, stability and prosperity (Banta, 1964), the dawn of the twentieth century also witnessed the emergence of several similar perceived threats to educators' autonomy, longevity, mobility and liberty (Au, 2011).

Shanley positions his fictional characters in a unique time of spiritual and political transition; his audience, though, watches these characters through a contemporary lens of educational and political reform. In both contexts, the respective stakeholders must confront their own doubts about where they came from and where they're going. *Doubt's* teacher-characters spend their narrative navigating the uncertainties of their Church's future, yet these same dramatic instruments also prompt real-life teachers to examine their roles in their respective schools, and how those roles (and those schools) are shifting in response to broad-sweeping political and national trends. Thus, insofar as it parabolizes schools and citizenship, *Doubt* also raises complex and poignant questions about what it truly means to leave no child behind.

This chapter investigates the conflicting depictions of teachers and teaching prevalent in *Doubt*. Because the parable couches education as a spiritual endeavor in its own rite, each of these characters serves as a sobering warning against conflating academic success with personal salvation. In particular, *Doubt* showcases the dangers that may surface when schools lose sight of their roles in children's lives and when teachers weaponize power in the name of self-preservation. In the midst of its governing indictments of moral corruption and clerical abuse, the inherent ambiguity of Shanley's narrative uniquely valorizes and demonizes these bastions of wisdom: Given the resonant lack of absolutes, each teacher can simultaneously operate as a villain, a hero, a sinner and a saint. As such, *Doubt* casts just as much speculation on the pious chastity of Father Flynn as it does about the pedagogical viability of his staff.

Reconciliation

Whereas *Doubt's* opening scene features only Father Flynn delivering a sermon mounted on the premise that "doubt can be a bond as powerful and sustaining as certainty" (Shanley, 2004, p. 14), the play's second scene introduces the two other pillars of St. Nicolas's trinity of troubled teachers. Sister Aloysius Beauvier, a "watchful, reserved, and unsentimental" (p. 14) woman in her 50s or 60s – and the principal of St. Nicolas – sits at her desk, soon joined by the much younger Sister James, a nun in her 20s with "a bit of sunshine in her heart" (p. 14). Without indulging in wasteful pleasantries, the two women quickly commence a layered critique of the questionable goings on of Sister James's classroom.

With little mercy, Sister Aloysius begins levying her concerns about Sister James's frustratingly liberal praxis, forcing the latter to defend herself and her progressive practice against her Superior's claims. The scene succeeds in establishing concrete binaries between these two equally ambitious, though woefully misaligned, educators.

Sister Aloysius grounds her teaching in suspicion, control, linearity and a strict, dogmatic loyalty to both her religious Order and the proper sequence of all things pertaining to her brand of education. Sister James, by contrast, refuses to succumb to her principal's cold, detached and skeptical view of students and schooling. The younger nun views her classroom as a collaborative space: a humanist, almost theatrical, enterprise comprised of teachers and students growing together and developing autonomy through their shared, authentic experiences.

Aloysius, however, opposes any implication that schools operate for any purpose other than to maintain the integrity and mission of the Church. According to the principal of St. Nicolas, everything that happens in a school – from student actions to teacher practice – must be assessed and handled according to the jurisdictions established by Those in Charge. For Aloysius, any deviation from this system, quite simply, is inappropriate.

Along these lines, despite its evident success with students, Aloysius makes no secret of her distain for James's playful pedagogical style. "The best teachers do not perform," she warns her subordinate; "They cause the students to perform" (Shanley, 2004, p. 17). Aloysius equates performance with an artificiality that borders on idolatry. She augments this mentality with her inherent distrust of popular lay leaders, like Franklin Roosevelt, whose widespread national appeal, she'd argue, masked his striking lack of Catholic zeal: "He was a good president, but he did not attempt to pack the Supreme Court. I do not approve of making heroes of lay historical figures" (p. 16).

Her aversion to history – or at least Sister James's "sugar-coating" (p. 16) of the subject – likely stems from her lived experience witnessing, first hand, the cataclysmic byproducts of charismatic men's pursuit of power. Because she lost her husband "in the war against Adolf Hitler" (p. 23) prior to taking her vows, Aloysius knows that no good comes when powerful men attempt to romanticize or otherwise make nostalgic selected elements of their own history in order to refurbish a forgotten (or fabricated) communal purpose or identity. This disdain for phallocentric egos – "boys," she laments, "are made of gravel, soot, and tar. Boys are a different breed" (p. 17) – coupled with her aversion to ambiguity, will ultimately fuel her campaign against Father Flynn and his insistence on using the pulpit as a mechanism for coercion and seduction.

And yet, at the same time, Aloysius rejects the saccharine lauding of the past – or, perhaps, people's blind devotion to their own flawed memories – she currently finds herself at a spiritual and pedagogical intersection. She may not love her church's/school's history but she certainly doesn't trust its future. She vocally bemoans the decline of vocations; she despises her younger colleagues' emphasis on art and music; and she stands at vehement odds against any secularized, modern attempt to simplify life for herself or her students. Passivity, in her calculated estimation, often shrouds corruption under a veneer of complacency and ease.

To this end, during this same initial conversation with Sister James, Aloysius recognizes Father Flynn's particular knack for "poetic" (Shanley, 2004, p. 19) speeches at the podium. Yet beneath her surfaced appreciation for Flynn's appealing presentational style lurks a not-so-subtle suggestion that the same tenet of his sermons that makes them otherwise engaging is precisely what compromises their sanctity. True value, she'd dispute, is hard and cannot be derived through satisfaction or simplicity, for in themselves, these demand no effort or sacrifice, intellectual or otherwise. It's always nice to just sit in a pew and listen; but that doesn't mean you're learning anything.

"Satisfaction is a vice," she relays to Sister James, after lamenting that "every easy choice today will have its consequence tomorrow. Mark my words" (p. 18). The fact that Sister James has already seemed to gather an impassioned student-following at Saint Nicolaus – that her kids actually *like* her – is a source of suspicion and disappointment for Principal Aloysius, who believes that all students should be "uniformly terrified" (p. 35) of their teachers. What Sister James offers her students in terms of compassion, love and a healthy, gentile acknowledgment of adolescent agency, her principal dismisses as simply the mark of an unbaptized Gentile, at least as teachers go. "You're showing off," she chides Sister James in their first scene together. "You like to see yourself ten feet tall in their eyes...The best teachers do not perform. They cause their students to perform" (p. 17).

"I feel I know how to handle them," (p. 18) James offers in humble defense.

"But perhaps you are wrong. And perhaps you are not working hard enough" (p. 18). Despite James's evident appeal with students and the fact that she certainly dresses the part, Aloysius knows that habits alone don't make the nun.

Ironically, it is this same "chain of discipline" (p. 18) by which Sister Aloysius seems intrinsically and unapologetically bound that also hitches her to an era looming on the cusp of obscurity. Just like the winds that perpetually plague her garden throughout the play, her Church/school, as purpose and place, is changing, and with it, by extension, are the needs and expectations of its students, teachers and the diverse community in which they each reside. It is these chains – shackles that have dually secured and squandered her success at St. Nicolas – that will ultimately crown her victory, or, like a crown of thorns, cap her eventual demise for a cause none but she may ever understand.

This introductory scene culminates with Sister Aloysius bestowing upon her novice colleague two distinct commandments of sorts. The first, and most pertinent to the play's plot, involves Sister James "keeping her wits" and being "alert" about "concerning matters at St. Nicolas:" to "see the starch in her character cultivated" so that she isn't fooled by any "wolf" (p. 20) preying to leverage her perception for their own personal gain.

The other, and far more tangential, directive involves another nun at the school, Sister Veronica, whom Sister Aloysius insists is going blind. Even though she has long been sheltered within the confines of her church, Aloysius fears that Veronica's failing vision will lead to her removal. "If they find out in the rectory, she'll be gone," Aloysius explains to Sister James; "If you see her making her way down those stone stairs into that courtyard, for the love of Heaven, lightly take her hand as if in fellowship and see that she doesn't destroy herself" (p. 20).

Even though Sister Veronica never appears in the play and is only referenced on two brief occasions, her inclusion in this scene illuminates that in Aloysius's capacity as a high-ranking member of a religious/academic Order, she recognizes that sight and perspective determine one's longevity. In a literal sense, Sister Veronica's worsening sight renders her unable to perform the tasks necessary for her position; symbolically, Sister Veronica highlights that churches and schools can shelter only those with depth perception, however faint and unreliable. If you can't see what's right in front of you, you don't belong in teaching.

That Sister Aloysius instructs Sister James to protect Sister Veronica only further demonstrates Aloysius's crusade for preservation, no matter how deceptive or impractical. "Her sight is fine. Nuns fall, you know," Aloysius dissimulates to Father Flynn after he seeks confirmation that Sister Veronica's sight is failing. "It's the habit. It catches up more often than not" (p. 28). As the play progresses, Sister Aloysius exemplifies just how far some nuns (and teachers) truly do fall, if not because of the obstruction of their outfits, then through their own reluctance to adapt them to the changing climate. Over time, some habits just lose their fit. Indeed, one of *Doubt's* most poignant comments on the field of education is its not-so-subtle insistence that classrooms often function as their own liturgical spaces, that under the ornate shrouds of policies, papacies, rites and rituals lurks, perhaps, a subversion that threatens to bring the whole messy, sacred system down.

Communion

The only scene in *Doubt* that features all three educators begins, in itself, as a lie.

After honoring her principal's instructions to pay more attention to her students, Sister James reports her concerns about a potentially inappropriate relationship between Father Flynn and Donald Miller, a new addition to the school and St. Nicolas's first African-American student. After returning from a private meeting with Father Flynn in the rectory, James recalls that Donald appeared detached and "frightened" (Shanley, 2004, p. 31). Reluctantly, and with oscillating conviction, Sister James confesses detecting alcohol on the boy's breath.

Despite Sister James's pleas that the two nuns address the situation through the proper institutional channels, Sister Aloysius maintains that the two must "stop him" themselves:

> The hierarchy of the Church does not permit my going to the Bishop," she justifies. "No. Once I tell the monsignor, it's out of my hands, I'm helpless. I'm going to have to come up with a pretext, get Father Flynn into my office. Try to force it.
>
> (p. 26)

The ensuing meeting begins innocently enough. Because Father Flynn believes that the impromptu conference involves the upcoming

Christmas pageant, he wastes no time expressing his plan to bring a little more fun to the show by adding secular songs to the program. In response to Sister James's youthful endorsement of "Frosty the Snowman," however, Sister Aloysius dismisses the song, insisting that it

> espouses a pagan belief in magic. The snowman comes to life when an enchanted hat is put on its head. If the music were more somber, people would realize the images are disturbing, and the song, heretical...It should be banned from the airwaves.
>
> (p. 30)

Father Flynn's desire to diversify the Christmas program signifies a dramatic shift in liturgical policy occurring between 1962 and 1965 (O'Malley, 2010). "I think the message of the Second Ecumenical Council was that the Church needs to take on a more familiar face," he defends to Sister Aloysius. "Reflect the local community. We should play a song from the radio now and then. Take the kids out for ice-cream" (Shanley, 2004, p. 30). In short, despite a nearly 2,000-year history of detachment, oppression and almost militaristic display of power and authority, Father Flynn echoes his Pope's contemporary calls that "we should be friendlier. The children and the parents should see us as members of their family and not emissaries from Rome" (p. 31).

"But we are not members of their family," Aloysius protests. "We're different" (p. 31). With this exchange, Shanley draws his line in the proverbial sand, relegating Conservation/Exclusion on one side and Progression/Inclusion on the other. Because she anchors her teaching in faith and religiosity, Aloysius embodies more of the Church; James, by contrast, serves as a more secular depiction of contemporary schools. Shanley then tethers these two paradigms through Father Flynn: the lush, though artificial garden that divides the rigid tradition of Aloysius's Church and the liberal secularism of James's school. "I don't come into this garden often," admits Sister Aloysius during one of her conversations with Sister James. "What is it, forty feet across? We might as well be separated by the Atlantic Ocean" (p. 23).

Inasmuch as Father Flynn embodies the conflicting religious symbol of the Garden itself – as a place of both innocence and temptation – by literally and symbolically parting the convent, rectory and school, he also serves as the bridge that unites the three. Yet while Sister Aloysius unapologetically maintains that "we are rightly discouraged from crossing paths with priests unattended" (p. 23), and thus, rarely ventures outside the parameters of her function and home, Sister James often finds herself in the garden, either alone with her thoughts or engaged in talks with Father Flynn. This subtle though decisive subversion of/in protocol marks a watershed moment that was reflective of the greater paradigm shift occurring in the Catholic Church during the 1960s.

The Second Ecumenical Council Father Flynn references (also known as the Second Vatican Council or, more colloquially, Vatican II) anchored a pivotal turning-point in Catholic tradition. As Teicher (2012) notes, Vatican II, "allowed for Catholics to pray with other Christian denominations, encouraged friendship with other non-Christian faiths, and opened the door for languages besides Latin to be used during Mass. Other new positions concerned education, the media and divine revelation" (NPR, 10/10/12). Of course, none of this sits well with Sister Aloysius. Much like today's veteran teachers who can recall, perhaps with bleached fondness, the peaceful times before No Child Left Behind, the beleaguered public servant must now reconcile an entire career spent preparing students according to X, with invasive decrees that now have her begging Why.

Sister James, however, experiences no such anxiety. Her cultural myopia and limited teaching experiences afford her the luxury of knowing no professional life outside the purview of Vatican II. Similar to how today's teachers have fewer memories of school free of excessive tests, teacher accountability or government takeovers, Sister James cannot conceive of a vocation that doesn't involve community outreach, cross-denominational dialogue and a renewed, modernized spirit of evangelical charity. And while, perhaps, the political undercurrents of these respective shifts are inverted – Vatican II sought to liberalize the Church through its modernized emphasis on community and equity (O'Malley, 2010), while No Child Left Behind (NCLB) is seen as a more conservative, seemingly "unjust" paradigm (Cobb & Rallis, 2008; Hamilton, Stecher, & Yuan, 2008) – the analogs of churches and schools and salvation and graduation remain, for the most part, intact.

In short, good works lead to salvation. A good Catholic life of service, sacrifice, humility and adoration will grant you riches in the afterlife. And a good academic life of service, sacrifice, humility and adoration will reap rewards in the after-school-life. Despite their variance on the political spectrum, both Vatican II and NCLB advocate for a paradigm in which "salvation" belongs solely to those who follow the Will of the Lord, however she/he/ they may manifest. And any teacher who has ever incentivized student cooperation – or otherwise shepherded their flock – through the premise and the promise that it would lead to success on the Test knows all too well the weight we put not only on the Test itself, whatever form it takes, but on the various Promised Lands our students may inhabit if and when they complete the Exodus of their education.

"It would be nice if this school weren't run like a prison!" (Shanley, 2004, p. 35) James exclaims to Aloysius in a moment of fleeting assertion. By play's end, though, James relinquishes this brief pursuit of self/preservation. She eventually concedes that Aloysius's crusade against Father Flynn has rendered her career as teacher and nun joyless, and her night without sleep. "I wish I could be like you..." she confesses to Aloysius in the play's closing lines. "Everything seems uncertain to me" (p. 51). Over time, Aloysius's staunch aversion to the figure and function of Father Flynn so chips away at the sophisticated tableau that James had sculpted for/with her students that, by the end of the play, the latter is but a puddle of her former self. Ironically, though, Shanley ends his play not with Sister James cowering in uncertainty to her superior's convictions but rather with Aloysius seeking consolation from her jaded novice, each having evidently been consumed with plaguing "such doubts" (p. 52).

Anointing of the Sick

Aside from the three educators, the only other speaking character in *Doubt* is Donald Miller's mother. Though she appears only in the play's penultimate scene, her inclusion in the play shines further light into the intricate caverns of Sister Aloysius's fissured sense of liturgical and academic accountability.

Principal Aloysius summons Mrs. Miller to the school to inform her of Father Flynn's seduction and abuse of her 12-year-old son. Mrs. Miller, however, is not persuaded to pursue justice. On the contrary, she seems content, even while appearing to believe Aloysius's claims, to keep Donald enrolled in school under the care of Father Flynn: "It's just till June," she excuses. "Sometimes things aren't black and white" (Shanley, 2004, p. 35).

While this scene ultimately serves to complicate Donald's character arc, as well as Aloysius's dilemma negotiating a suitable recourse for Donald and Father Flynn, it also positions St. Nicolas – as both church and school – in communion with the greater world. Whereas in the previous scenes, St. Nicolas has remained distinct and detached from its neighboring community, Mrs. Miller's arrival bridges the gap between the liturgical space of the classroom and the civic realm of the external world. She offers the singular voice of the lay community, thus humanizing the congregation with which Father Flynn so eagerly seeks connection and the population from which Aloysius so earnestly wishes detachment. Mrs. Miller sees the school the way her community sees it: broken, corrupt, small, cold. But also necessary. It may be full of broken, corrupt people but they are people who also do good, people who protect, "who have their reasons," (p. 45) yes, but who help the children get where they need to go. Being abused by a man who cares is better than being killed by a man who doesn't, as long as Donald comes out the other side.

Ultimately, what Mrs. Miller serves to disrupt is Aloysius's pride in and conception of her entire spiritual and pedagogical vocation. What really is the point of school, she forces Aloysius to consider, or of faith in general? Despite her brief presence on stage, Mrs. Miller is arguably the pivotal figure in the play. Her destruction of the various barriers between St. Nicolas and the community render Sister Aloysius in the unique, though vulnerable, position of having to reconcile her professional and spiritual existence not only with a stakeholder but also with herself. Perhaps as a nod to Sister Veronica and her fledging sight, Mrs. Miller's conversation with her son's principal forces the latter to confront her own myopic condition and come to terms with her inability to navigate the external world from which she's exiled herself for years. She now may know what the world knows and see what the world sees but such knowledge doesn't come without shame.

By the play's conclusion, Aloysius begins to see her school through the same lens as Mrs. Miller. In finally soldering herself to the people she's spent a career avoiding, she now gazes back upon her sanctuary with the clarity of a citizen capable of seeing its cracks. So, when faced with the choice of removing Donald Miller from the school – defying his mother's wishes while likely saving him from the clutches of a "dog that bites" (p. 49) – she hesitates. As with Mrs. Miller, Principal Aloysius knows that despite her school's flaws – its brokenness and corruption and smallness and cold – kids are better off with a diploma than without one. And even though some nuns may fall and some priests touch kids, following God will be worth it in the end.

Last Rites

"You make up little stories to illustrate. In the tradition of the parable," Father Flynn tells Sister James in the garden that separates the church and the school. "What actually happens in life is beyond interpreting. The truth makes a bad sermon. It tends to be confusing and have no clear conclusion" (Shanley, 2004, p. 37). And indeed, when it comes to *Doubt,* truer words are never spoken.

We never meet Donald Miller. Instead, we must view him solely through the eyes of his teachers, those charged with formally preparing him for the world that one day awaits him, and the woman who first brought him into the world. Shanley intentionally shields us from the boy, perhaps as a means of depersonalizing (or dehumanizing) the educative exchange. Or maybe we never meet Donald simply because the play was never really about him in the first place. Donald Miller is a symptom, a cough or hiccup in an otherwise well-oiled machine, an unnerving reminder that every system has flaws and even beautiful gardens sometimes have snakes.

We never learn what happened in the rectory but maybe it never mattered. Nor do we ever learn why Sister Aloysius concludes her role "bent with tears," weeping about "such doubts" (p. 52). But we can't believe that her uncertainties end with Father Flynn. As complex and contradictory representations of education stakeholders, these characters are nothing if not each tragically resistant to simplicity, despite their subconscious longing for it.

Sister James, for example, personifies pedagogical naivety, the teacher whose blind idealism is abruptly and painfully eclipsed by the harsh realities of a schooled-life banished from the innocence of Edenic college methods courses. Her counterpart, Sister Aloysius, embodies the extension of James's unraveling: the Post-Eden Eve. She finds herself lost in her own wilderness, mirrored by any teacher who's ever questioned the viability of their pursuit and who, rather than succumb to the truth of their own finitude (or ineptitude), may find solace in their condemnation of the various cogs in the machine they helped build. It's always easier to blame

Father Flynn for being evil than curse God for being absent – or worse, non-existent.

Churches have always ordained Father Flynns, and schools will forever ward off wolf-like teachers who prey on their sheep. It's dangerously simple to reduce Aloysius's parting anguish to an admonishment of one man's imperfections. The darker and perhaps far more scathing alternative is that Aloysius fades to black under crippling doubts about the System itself: the same system against which she spent the entirety of the play fighting but without which she'd cease to exist.

And so, Shanley ends his parable with us in the garden, wandering and wondering not only if Father Flynn is guilty or if Aloysius will quit the Church or if James will ever sleep again. Shanley plants his garden between his church and his school: two distinct but linked institutions built on the premise that good works and humble submission lead to a better life. Both demand sacrifice and grit and effort, and both demand the loyal labors of men and women who take up the call.

Shanley's garden is a place of possibilities and hope, love and tenderness and beauty. But like Eden, it's also a place of shame, power and isolation, of greed and evil and doubt. As an audience, Shanley challenges us all to determine for ourselves not only which garden to inhabit and which school to attend, but also which paradigm logically follows the other. Though his teachers can never escape the liminal space between the church and school – that idyllic realm where knowledge grows on trees and snakes make us do bad things – Shanley does grant us the chance (and burden) of choosing who and what and how to believe. Thus, like the Bible itself or the spirit of any Commencement ceremony, *Doubt* leaves us all at the beginning: sitting on a bench or in a pew or by a row of desks or in the Principal's office, alone with our thoughts and prayers, silently asking ourselves who we are, where we came from, why we're here and what we do when we're just not sure.

References

Au, W. (2011). Teaching under the new Taylorism: High-stakes testing and the standardization of 21st century curriculum. *Journal of Curriculum Studies*, 43(1), 25–45.

Banta, T. (1964). The Kennedy assassination: Early thoughts and emotions. *Public Opinion Quarterly*, 28(2), 216–224.

Cobb, C. D., & Rallis, S. F. (2008). District responses to NCLB: Where is the justice? *Leadership and Policy in Schools*, 7(2), 178–201.

Hamilton, L. S., Stecher, B. M., & Yuan, K. (2008). *Standards-based reform in the United States: History, research, and future directions.* Washington, DC: RAND Corporation.

O'Malley, J. (2010). *What happened at Vatican II?* New York: Belknap Press.

Rezendes, M. (2002). Church allowed abuse by priests for years. *Boston Globe*, January 6. "Spotlight Report."

Shanley, J. P. (2004). *Doubt: A parable.* New York: Dramatists Play Service Inc.

Teicher, J. G. (2012). Why is Vatican II so important? *Religion: NPR.* Retrieved from https://www.npr.org/2012/10/10/162573716/why-is-vatican-ii-so-important

Response to Chapter 7
Faith and Futurity: Embracing the Struggle

Julie Gorlewski

"A Holey Trinity" presents a view of teachers as well-intentioned but disempowered. They exercise power within the system but fail to perceive how they are enacting relations of power that emanate from the institution they serve. Characters embody conflicts without recognizing how they shape, and are shaped by, their society and its norms, and they relentlessly seek certainty and resolution. In some ways, then, their concentration on clear resolution of problems dooms them to futility. Echoing the drama, in which Father Flynn states that "doubt can be a bond as powerful and sustaining as certainty" (Shanley, 2004, p. 14), I argue that *struggle can be a bond as powerful as conciliation*, and struggle is more likely to tend toward equity. Therefore, I encourage today's educators to focus on futurity, in faith that this orientation will cultivate the promise of justice.

Social institutions, like the church portrayed in Shanley's *Doubt*, embody and reflect existing relations of power; as such, their default pursuits necessarily tend toward reproduction of the status quo. Although social institutions claim to be answerable to society, in reality, political structures result in their being accountable to the dominant cultural and political forces. In fact, if society were just and equitable, it would be appropriate to reproduce existing conditions. However, in an unjust society constructed by imperfect humans, social institutions must seek change, even as they enact rituals and traditions that replicate historical circumstances. In essence, then, Spanke's chapter calls into question the purpose of schooling, an issue that continues to be a source of enduring societal tensions. The matter can be considered temporally: Do schools exist to serve the past, the present or the future? On the surface, this may seem to beg an obvious answer: Schools should serve the future, since it would be pointless to serve a bygone time or a fleeting moment. In reality, though, as evidenced through policy and practice, education is rarely oriented toward the future and, even less, toward *futurity* (Kuttner, 2017) – a concept that is likely unfamiliar to many educators. This concept, rooted in Indigenous epistemologies, offers a means of reimagining competing beliefs regarding the purposes of education and may provide a framework for teachers to enact conflicting roles with ethical integrity.

Through characters identified as teachers, "A Holey Trinity" explores conflicts inherent in the practice of teaching. For example, Spanke presents the dichotomous approaches of Sister Aloysius and Sister James as oriented toward preservation and transformation, respectively. Contrasting preservation and transformation is a helpful exercise, but it also diminishes attention toward an alternative path, one that integrates the past and the present and also focuses on "*future* as an arena of active struggle" (Kuttner, 2017, n.p.). An integrated temporal understanding is grounded in a collective intention: that teachers work today in order to prepare learners to construct a better, more just future. This is fundamentally associated with futurity:

> The concept of futurity implies active struggle tomorrow which requires that educators engage in active struggle, with their learners, today. To cultivate the possibility of constructing a more just future, learners need to experience what it means to challenge injustice and to question the status quo. The work of teachers can reinforce the status quo, shaping a future that resembles the present, or it can pursue transformation – establishing an environment wherein educators work with students to imagine and create a society in which the struggle toward justice is habitual.
>
> (Gorlewski & Tuck, 2019, p. 186)

In many ways, teachers serve as agents of the state. Teacher salaries are paid by tax dollars; their positions depend on public support, both materially and philosophically. Teaching credentials and licensure requirements are built on existing systems of knowledge and authority. As part of institutions that confer credentials, they are charged to enable students to earn diplomas, certificates and post-secondary credits. Through these efforts, the state depends on teachers to prepare professionals in all fields, as well as to coach learners to become active, engaged citizens who participate in the public sphere. In short, teachers are part of a system that depends on us to produce an educated populace. In these ways, teachers are agents of the state who maintain the status quo.

But teachers are also agents of change, who perceive the purposes of education as transformative. In this capacity, teachers connect classroom practices to broader social issues. They engage in credentialing activities but consider how these perpetuate existing inequities and strive to interrupt processes that do so. Teachers are paid to serve the state but seek change as a moral imperative, often as an avocation. Questioning the status quo is not what teachers are paid to do; however, by definition, agents of change aim to disrupt the status quo. Public educators clearly enact complex, sometimes contradictory, roles. To be an agent of the state is an institutional mandate. To be an agent of change is a moral imperative. Teachers are asked to walk at once on two divergent paths; to serve only as an agent of the state requires ethical educators to disavow knowledge (Taubman, 2012) of their ultimate answerability to learners. This duality reveals the fact that, whether or not we recognize it as such, teaching is political work. Choices teachers – and leaders in any social institution, including churches – make in their daily work reflect whether they are agents of the state or agents of change.

This tension between our working to support today's society and preparing learners to construct a better future requires both faith and doubt. Teachers, as products of traditional educational systems and as agents of the state, represent historical conventions and are expected to uphold institutional norms. In addition, they are expected to support these institutions to endeavor to transform toward equity and justice. Educators embody faith in the existing system and doubt in its adequacy. Doubts raise questions about contemporary society; to question a system from within that system requires faith in its integrity. Moreover, the work of teaching rests on faith in the future – in the young people whose minds, hearts and spirits we seek to cultivate to construct a more just and equitable world. To do this, we must foster confidence in the system (and in us, as educators) as well as develop critical dispositions as the tools necessary to interrupt structural oppression. As Spanke (2019) notes,

> *Doubt* showcases the dangers that may surface when schools lose sight of their roles in children's lives and when teachers weaponize power in the name of self-preservation. In the midst

of its governing indictments of moral corruption and clerical abuse, the inherent ambiguity of Shanley's narrative uniquely valorizes and demonizes these bastions of wisdom: Given the resonant lack of absolutes, each teacher can simultaneously operate as a villain, a hero, a sinner and a saint.

(p. 105)

Social institutions are, in many ways, "corrupt, small, cold" (Spanke, 2019, p. 113) and old, but they are also a ramp to future possibilities. They are mechanisms of exclusion and instruments of opportunity. Obliteration of existing systems, however flawed, is not a solution.

As professionals who are part of the education system, teachers must navigate – and, in their lived experiences, integrate – dual roles: simultaneously acting as agents of the state and agents of change. Like Sister Aloysius and Sister James, teachers must inhabit different places along this agentive continuum of state and change as they try to improve the lives of learners. Living with(in) and embracing conflict is not a condition that is comfortable for many educators, however. As Jones (2007) explains (Gorlewski & Tuck, 2018), public education in Western societies has enacted a problem-solution approach to educating young people. Such an approach involves identifying gaps, deficits and crises, and then seeking ways that schools can tackle and resolve them. Among other concerns, a problem-solution perspective (1) is hierarchical rather than dialogic, (2) preconceives what counts as knowledge and (3) establishes learners as empty vessels rather than active participants. These drawbacks result in learning experiences that foster disengagement, rather than engagement:

> Engagement, according to Jones (2007), is more complex, meaningful, and useful than the problem-solution approach. Engagement implies connection, but it does not require compliance. In fact, engagement privileges the struggles that occur within relationships, because engagement is preferable to disengagement. She explains: "we are *engaged* in a relationship. This has to be seen positively, given it *is engagement*; it is not *dis*-engagement. To struggle with another is to give active and proper *attention* to the other, to *relate* to the other" (p. 12).
>
> (Gorlewski & Tuck, 2018, p. 28)

In order to act with integrity and to be answerable to learners, teachers must focus on futurity, which requires belief in engagement as ongoing struggle. We must trust young people and doubt those in power, and we must demonstrate faith that the construction of a more just world is possible. To do this, educators must traverse dual paths; but how? I suggest that this struggle is an internal conflict that we must embody by approaching our work by integrating two lenses: critical compliance and reflective resistance. That is, we can be both agents of the state and agents of change by examining professional dilemmas and considering these possibilities. Teachers can *comply* with mandates necessary for students to earn credentials but they can comply critically rather than silently, amplifying unjust circumstances alongside students. Similarly, when conditions allow, teachers can *resist* unjust policies, but do so thoughtfully, collectively and publicly. If wise and caring teachers lose their jobs on principle, their replacements may well contribute to increasing educational inequalities. Public pedagogies are essential to lift shrouds of secrecy and opacity that enable injustices to be perpetuated. These paths enable educators to avoid dichotomous paths and embrace futurity so that today's learners are prepared and positioned to build a more just and equitable tomorrow.

References

Gorlewski, J. A., & Tuck, E. (2018). *Who decides who becomes a teacher? Schools of education as sites of resistance.* New York: Routledge.

Kuttner, P. (2017). Futurism, futurity, and the importance of the existential imagination. *Cultural Organizing.* Retrieved from http://culturalorganizing.org/futurism-futurity/

Shanley, J. P. (2004). *Doubt: A parable.* New York: Dramatists Play Service Inc.

Taubman, P. M. (2012). *Disavowed knowledge: Psychoanalysis, education, and teaching.* New York: Routledge.

Index

126   *Index*